I0438904

Inventory of Exotic Plant Species Occurring in Salinas Pueblo Missions National Monument

Natural Resource Technical Report NPS/SCPN/NRTR—2011/422

Julie E. Korb
Biology Department
Fort Lewis College
1000 Rim Drive
Durango, CO 81301

January 2011

U.S. Department of the Interior
National Park Service
Natural Resource Program Center
Fort Collins, Colorado

The National Park Service, Natural Resource Program Center publishes a range of reports that address natural resource topics of interest and applicability to a broad audience in the National Park Service and others in natural resource management, including scientists, conservation and environmental constituencies, and the public.

The Natural Resource Technical Report Series is used to disseminate results of scientific studies in the physical, biological, and social sciences for both the advancement of science and the achievement of the National Park Service mission. The series provides contributors with a forum for displaying comprehensive data that are often deleted from journals because of page limitations.

All manuscripts in the series receive the appropriate level of peer review to ensure that the information is scientifically credible, technically accurate, appropriately written for the intended audience, and designed and published in a professional manner.

Views, statements, findings, conclusions, recommendations, and data in this report do not necessarily reflect views and policies of the National Park Service, U.S. Department of the Interior. Mention of trade names or commercial products does not constitute endorsement or recommendation for use by the U.S. Government.

This project was funded by the National Park Service through the Colorado Plateau CESU, Cooperative Agreement #H1200-004-0002 (Task FLC-14).

This report is available from the Southern Colorado Plateau Network (http://science.nature.nps.gov/im/units/scpn/) and the Natural Resource Publications Management Web site (http://www.nature.nps.gov/publications/NRPM) on the Internet.

The corresponding author and project manager for this project is Julie Korb (korb_j@fortlewis.edu). Sensa Watkins and Ben Wolcott were the botanists for this project. Other contributions were made by the SCPN staff.

Please cite this publication as:

Korb, J. E. 2011. Inventory of exotic plant species occurring in Salinas Pueblo Missions National Monument. Natural Resource Technical Report NPS/SCPN/NRTR—2011/422. National Park Service, Fort Collins, Colorado.

Contents

Figures

Tables

Introduction and Background

Exotic plant species are invading over 70,000 ha (172,973 ac) of United States habitats per year (Pimentel 2004). Exotic species are a leading cause of biodiversity loss and rank second only to habitat destruction in causing species endangerment across the US (Brooks and Pyle 2001). Exotic species invasions have been a primary cause in the listing of over 400 species as threatened or endangered under the Endangered Species Act (Pimentel 2004). These invasions have contributed to the fragmentation to native ecosystems, displacement of native plants and animals, and alterations to ecosystem function. National parks are not immune to exotic plant species' negative impacts on natural resources and visitor experience. Exotic plant species modify landscapes and natural disturbance regimes, such as fire and flooding, reduce native plant and animal habitat, and increase trail maintenance needs (Young et al. 2007). For national parks in the Southern Colorado Plateau Inventory and Monitoring Network (SCPN), the first step to controlling exotic plants is to complete an exotic species inventory. The inventory results may then be combined with other information to prioritize exotic species for control based on their invasiveness and/or feasibility of control and to prioritize park areas for control based on their conservation status and/or restoration potential.

Project area

Salinas Pueblo Missions National Monument is located in central New Mexico near the town of Mountainair. Gran Quivira was established as a National Monument in 1909, with Abo and Quarai park units established in 1980 (NPS 1984). The three units were redesignated as Salinas Pueblo Missions National Monument in 1987. The Monument was established to "set apart and preserve for the benefit and enjoyment of the American People the ruins of prehistoric Indian pueblos and associated seventeenth century Franciscan Spanish mission ruins" (NPS 2006). The Monument offers visitors an opportunity to experience the physical remains of prehistoric cultures.

Visitation at Salinas Pueblo Missions National Monument has decreased slightly over the last decade.

However, increased growth rates of Albuquerque and the Rio Grande Basin will likely increase visitation in the future. Approximately 35,000 people visited the Monument in 2005 for recreational purposes. The busiest months for visitation to the monument are July and October (NPS 2006). Humans are one of the main vectors for exotic plant species dispersal; therefore increased human use may result in increases in exotic species.

Project overview

The specific objectives of this project were to complete an exotic plant inventory, collect voucher specimens for new exotic species in the park, and write a report on exotic plant species occurring in Salinas Pueblo Missions National Monument. This information may then be incorporated into future weed management projects to restore and preserve the vegetation and cultural landscape.

Methods

Study area

We conducted the inventory at Salinas Pueblo Missions National Monument in the high desert plains of east-central New Mexico. The monument is located in the foothills of the Manzano Mountains in the Estancia Basin. Elevations in the monument range between 1,826 m (5,990 ft) to 2,046 m (6,713 ft).The monument is relatively small in size, consisting of approximately 445 ha (1,100 ac) of land divided into three separate units (Gran Quivira, Abo, and Quarai) (USDOI 2004). The area consists of Permian sedimentary deposits of sandstone and limestone interlayered with gravel and conglomerates. The broad valleys and undrained depressions are covered by Quaternary alluvium to a considerable depth. Gray San Andres limestone outcrops at Gran Quivira provided building material for mission and pueblo construction. Abo sandstone and shale was used for construction at Abo and Quarai. The soils at the three units comprise seven soil types: Alicia loam, Chupadera loamy fine sand, Encierro channery loam, La Fonda loam, Manzano loam, Otero and Palma soils,

Figure 1. The dominant vegetation in the Gran Quivira park unit includes oneseed juniper, cholla, and four-wing saltbush.

Figure 2. In the Abo park unit, grama grasses and oneseed juniper dominate the vegetation.

Figure 3. The Quarai park unit includes a grove of cottonwoods and willows.

and Witt loam. These are generally loamy fine sands on the surface and are of shallow to deep depth, with rapid permeability and low moisture-holding capacity. They are generally unstable, with both wind and water erosion occurring at all three units. Soil erosion occurs where vegetation cover is sparse and slopes are steep; these areas are especially prone to erosion from surface runoff during storms (USDOI 2004).

The dominant vegetation in the three units consists of pinyon-juniper woodland and juniper woodland or savanna. The dominant species at Gran Quivira are oneseed juniper (*Juniperus monosperma.*), walking stick cholla (*Opuntia imbricata*), four-wing saltbush (*Artiplex canescens*), and various species of yucca (*Yucca* spp.)(USDOI 2004)(fig. 1). Gran Quivira sits atop Chupadera Mesa and has no perennial water sources; therefore, the vegetation is homogenous. The Abo and Quarai units both have small perennial water sources; therefore the vegetation is slightly more diverse. At Abo, the vegetation is dominated by grama grasses (*Bouteloua* spp.), cholla, and oneseed juniper (fig. 2). Quarai, with its more abundant water, is dominated by cholla but also contains a grove of cottonwoods (*Populus fremontii*), willows (*Salix lutea*), and wild roses (*Rosa* spp.)(USDOI 2004)(fig. 3).

Sampling design

This inventory is one of several exotic plant inventories that have been conducted in NPS units of the Southern Colorado Plateau Network (SCPN). For each, sampling followed a systematic, grid-based approach (Young et al. 2007) to ensure rapid and repeatable data collection. The SCPN Spatial Analyst created a gridded map of the park property, resulting in over 200 grid cells, each approximately 125 X 160 m (2 ha) in area. Irregular polygons were reshaped to create consistency in grid unit size and search efficiency. Within each grid cell, a diagonal 50-m transect, along which we collected vegetation and environmental data, was mapped through the cell center. The SCPN Spatial Analyst randomly selected 125 grid cells to inventory for exotic plants in the three park units: Abo, Gran Quivira, and Quarai (table 1) (fig. 4). We conducted the inventory from mid June

Land Cover Types

Land Cover Types
- Grassland
- PJ Woodland
- PJ Woodland and Savanna
- Riparian
- Riparian Shrubland
- Shrubland
- Sparsely Vegetated
- Urban
- Area Not Inventoried

Quarai

Abo

Gran Quivira

Figure 4. Map of the sampled cells by land cover type for the exotic plant inventory. Each grid cell was approximately 2 ha each. One 50-m transect was sampled within each cell.

Table 1. Number of grid cells for each land cover type in each park unit at Salinas Pueblo Missions National Monument.

Park unit	Land cover type	Number of grid cells
Abo	PJ Woodland and Savanna	17
	PJ Woodland	8
	Grassland	8
	Riparian	1
	Riparian Shrubland	1
	Sparsely Vegetated	1
Gran Quivira	PJ Woodland and Savanna	39
	PJ Woodland	29
	Shrubland	5
	Urban	2
	Sparsely Vegetated	1
	Grassland	1
Quarai	PJ Woodland and Savanna	4
	Grassland	3
	PJ Woodland	2
	Riparian	2
	Sparsely Vegetated	1

to mid September in 2009.

Field methods

The field crew consisted of two botanists. We used a Garmin GPS unit that was pre-programmed with mapping coordinates for all 125 grid cells and 50-m transects to navigate to all grid cells and transect locations. We marked all transect beginning and ending points with the GPS in order to verify the transect locations. The SCPN also provided us with a paper map, which we used to reference known ground features and structures for orientation.

Vegetation

The field crew became familiar with both the exotic and native species occurring within the monument prior to conducting the inventory. We used species lists compiled by Salinas Pueblo Missions National Monument and SCPN as botanical references. The botanists collected any unknown species in a plant press and identified them to the species level. The five species we determined to be exotic that were not listed on the previously compiled lists, were photographed, marked with the GPS system, and collected in a plant press for voucher specimens. We collected and carefully pressed the best specimens, ideally those with fruit, flower, and leaves.

We classified each of the 125 grid cells into one of eight land cover types: Grassland, Pinyon-Juniper Woodland, Pinyon-Juniper Woodland and Savanna, Riparian, Riparian Shrubland, Shrubland, Sparsely Vegetated, and Urban (table 1). These are vegetation land types that were established by Salinas Pueblo Missions National Monument staff. We established a variable width belt along each 50-m transect using a 3-m belt width in areas that were in the Grassland land cover type, a 4-m belt width in the Pinyon-Juniper Woodland and Savanna, and a 7-m transect for all other land cover types. The botanist documented the exotic species along the 50-m variable width belt transect and assigned a cover class for each exotic species. We assigned exotic species found within the variable width belt a cover class using the following cover class system: 1=less than 0.1% foliar cover, 2=0.1 to 1%, 3=1 to 5%, 4=5 to10%, 5=10 to 25%, 6=25 to 50%, and 7=50 to 100%. We then used the GPS to walk the perimeter and the area within the entire grid cell to identify any additional exotic species found within the grid cell but not within the 50-m variable width belt transect.

Environmental measures

We also determined if any environmental variables correlated with the presence of exotic plant species. We recorded transect aspect, slope, tree canopy cover, bare soil, and soil disturbance. We recorded aspect at the 25-meter mark using a compass. We measured the slope using a clinometer from the 0-m mark looking towards the 50-m mark. One observer stood at the 0-m mark and the other at the 50-m mark. In areas where the topography was inconsistent, a reading was taken from 0-25 meters and then from 25-50 meters and averaged. We estimated tree canopy cover using a spherical densiometer every 10 m, starting at the 5-m mark along transects. We quantified soil disturbance by the amount of organic soil that had been removed in a given area, using the following soil disturbance scale: 1=bladed road, 2=heavy disturbance where more than 75% of the organic soil had been removed, 3=intermediate disturbance where 40-75% of the organic soil has been removed, 4=light disturbance where less than 45% of organic soil has been removed, and 5=where there is no disturbance (Korb et al. 2007). The observer took four photographs in each grid cell at the 25-m mark: one photograph from 25-0 meters, one photograph from 25-50 meters, and two photographs that represented the general vegetation and geographical features of the grid cell. We also photographed any human disturbances or unique features within each grid cell.

Statistical data summary

The SCPN Data Manager designed the Microsoft Access database and queries used to summarize the inventory data. We entered the data into the database, verified all data records, and made corrections as needed. We analyzed data using SAS JMP-IN Version 7 and used Microsoft Excel to create tables and figures. The SCPN Spatial Analyst designed GIS maps displaying the spatial distribution of exotic species within the monument.

We calculated the percent exotic cover by calculating a midpoint for each cover class and then calculating the means from the midpoint data (N=125). We calculated the frequency by adding the number of grid cells for any given individual exotic species and dividing it by the total number of belt transects in the monument. For example, if a species was present in all 125 belt transects it would have a frequency of 100 percent. If a species was present in 75 belt transects, it would have a frequency of 60 percent.

Results

Plant cover

Total exotic plant cover in Salinas Pueblo Missions National Monument was 2.5%.

Convolvulus arvensis (field bindweed) had the highest overall plant cover, averaging 1.26% (table 2). Two other exotic species had an average plant cover over a quarter percent: *Kochia scoparia* (common kochia) averaged 0.77%, and *Marrubium vulgare* (horehound) averaged 0.37% (table 2).

Grid cell 187 in the Grassland land cover type had the highest exotic cover of 75.05%, with two species on the transect: *Convolvulus arvensis* (75%) and *Kochia scoparia* (0.05%) (appendix A). Grid cell 192 in the Grassland land cover type and grid cell 197 in the Riparian land cover type had the second highest exotic cover of 38.6%, each with five species in the grid cell; *Convolvulus arvensis* (37.5%) made up the majority of the cover in both grid cells (appendix A). Grid cell 20 in the Grassland land cover type had the third highest exotic cover of 37.55%, with two species in the grid cell: *Kochia sco-*

Table 2. Average percent cover for individual exotic plant species and frequency in Salinas Pueblo Missions National Monument.

Species	Common name	Cover (%)	Frequency (%)
Convolvulus arvensis	field bindweed	**1.2612**	**5.6**
Kochia scoparia	common kochia	**0.7652**	**8.8**
Marrubium vulgare	horehound	**0.3656**	**10.4**
Melilotus officinalis	yellow sweetclover	0.0200	5.6
Rumex crispus	curly dock	0.0200	4
Poa pratensis	Kentucky bluegrass	0.0092	4
Bromus catharticus	rescue brome	0.0080	2.4
Salsola tragus	prickly Russian thistle	0.0064	7.2
Lactuca serriola	wild lettuce	0.0040	0.8
Taraxacum officinale	common dandelion	0.0008	3.2
Tragopogon dubius	western goat's beard	0.0004	4
Bromus japonicus	Japanese brome	0.0004	1.6
Sisymbrium altissimum	Jim Hill mustard	0.0004	0.8
Erodium cicutarium	redstem stork's bill	0.0004	4.8
Carduus nutans	nodding plumeless thistle	0	0.8
Eleusine indica	bermuda grass	0	0.8
Malus pumila	apple tree	0	0.8
Malva neglecta	cheeseweed	0	0.8
Medicago lupulina	black medic	0	0.8
Tamarix spp.	tamarisk	0	3.2
Ulmus pumila	Siberian elm	0	2.4

Note: The three exotic species with over a quarter average percent cover for the entire monument are in bold.

paria (37.5%) and *Poa pratensis* (0.05%) (appendix A). Grid cells 39, 192, and 197 also all had cover values of 37.5 (appendix A).

Cover by park unit

The Quarai park unit had the highest average exotic plant cover with 14.42% (fig. 5). *Convolvulus arvensis* had 12.51% average cover and *Kochia scoparia* with 1.67% (table 3). The Abo park unit had the second highest average exotic plant cover with 2.49% (fig. 5). *Kochia scoparia* had 2.1% average cover (table 3). The Gran Quivira park unit had the

lowest average exotic plant cover with 0.59% (fig. 5), all of which was *Marrubium vulgare* (table 3).

Cover by land cover types

The Grassland land cover type had the highest average exotic plant cover with 17.49% (fig. 6). *Convolvulus arvensis* had 9.38% average cover, followed by *Kochia scoparia* with 7.97 (table 4). The Riparian land cover type had the second highest average exotic plant cover with 17.47% (fig. 6). *Convolvulus arvensis* had 15.02% average cover (table

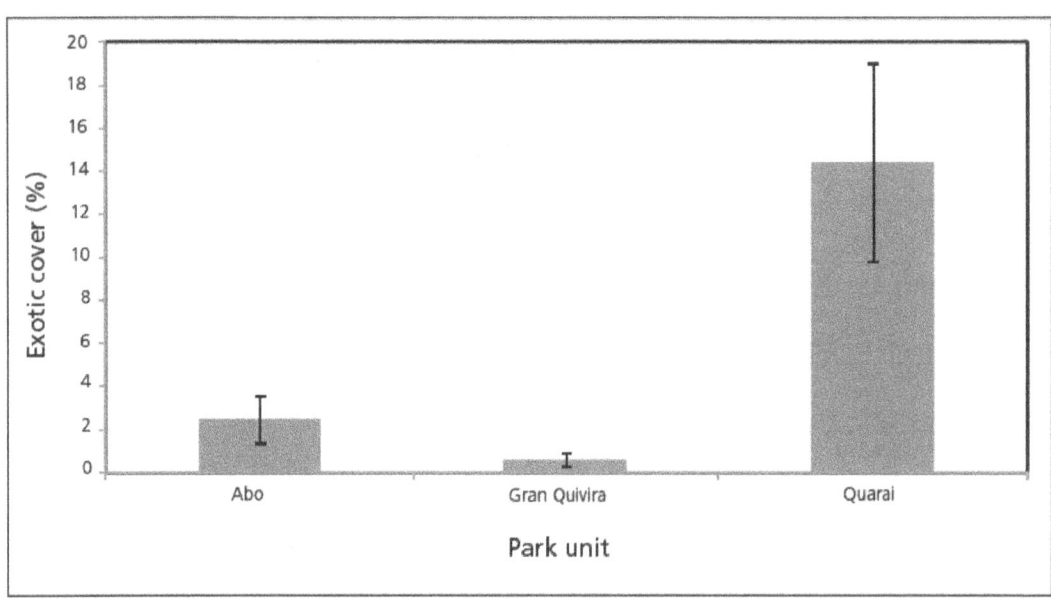

Figure 5. Mean exotic plant cover for each park unit. Error bars represent ±SEM.

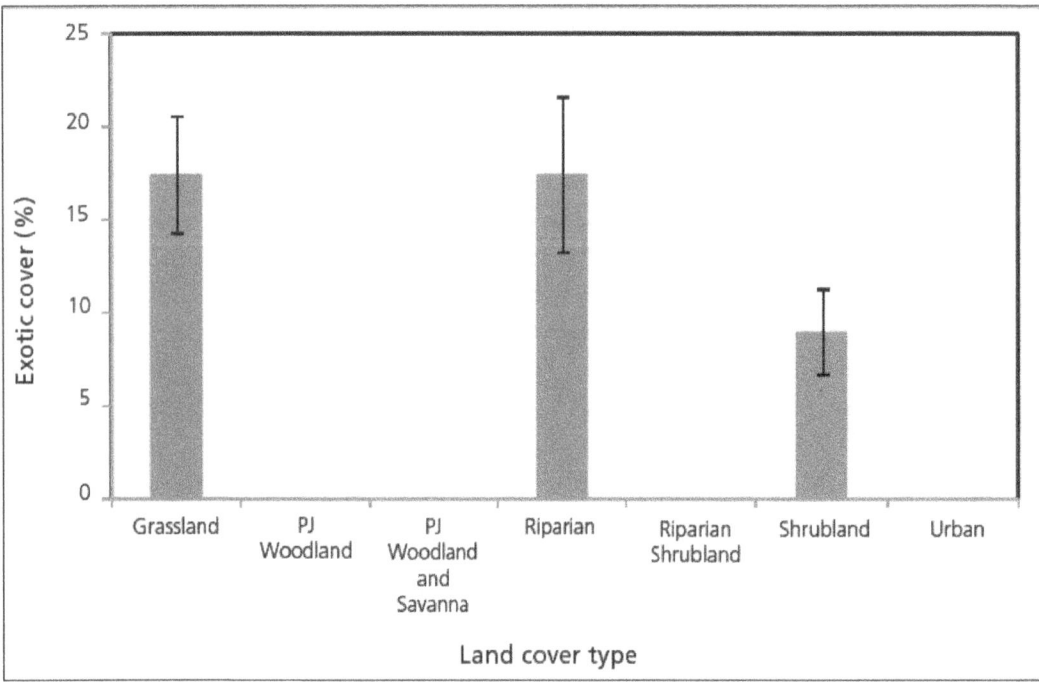

Figure 6. Mean exotic plant cover by land cover type using 50-m belt transect data. Belt transect width varied in size depending on land cover type. Error bars represent ±SEM.

Table 3. Average percent cover for exotic plant species by park unit in Salinas Pueblo Missions National Monument.

Park unit	Species	Common name	Cover (%)	Frequency (%)
Abo	*Kochia scoparia*	common kochia	2.100	19.44
	Convolvulus arvensis	field bindweed	0.210	5.56
	Rumex crispus	curly dock	0.069	8.33
	Melilotus officinalis	yellow sweetclover	0.069	13.89
	Salsola tragus	prickly Russian thistle	0.019	16.67
	Bromus catharticus	rescue brome	0.014	5.56
	Poa pratensis	Kentucky bluegrass	0.003	5.56
	Taraxacum officinale	common dandelion	0.001	5.56
	Sisymbrium altissimum	Jim Hill mustard	0.001	2.78
	Marrubium vulgare	horehound	0.001	8.33
	Erodium cicutarium	redstem stork's bill	0.001	8.33
	Tamarix spp.	tamarisk	0	11.11
	Tragopogon dubius	western goat's beard	0	5.56
	Ulmus pumila	Siberian elm	0	5.56
	Carduus nutans	nodding plumeless thistle	0	2.78
	Eleusine indica	goose grass	0	2.78
Gran Quivira	*Marrubium vulgare*	horehound	0.593	12.99
Quarai	*Convolvulus arvensis*	field bindweed	12.508	41.67
	Kochia scoparia	common kochia	1.671	33.33
	Poa pratensis	Kentucky bluegrass	0.0900	25
	Lactuca serriola	wild lettuce	0.042	8.33
	Bromus tectorum	cheat grass	0.042	25.00
	Bromus catharticus	rescue grass	0.040	8.33
	Salsola tragus	prickly Russian thistle	0.008	25.00
	Melilotus officinalis	yellow sweetclover	0.008	16.67
	Tragopogon dubius	western goat's beard	0.004	25.00
	Taraxacum officinale	common dandelion	0.004	16.67
	Bromus japonicus	Japanese brome	0.004	16.67
	Erodium cicutarium	redstem stork's bill	0	25.00
	Rumex crispus	curly dock	0	16.67
	Malus pumila	apple tree	0	8.33
	Malva neglecta	cheeseweed	0	8.33
	Medicago lupulina	black medic	0	8.33
	Ulmus pumila	Siberian elm	0	8.33

Table 4. Average percent cover for exotic plant species by land cover type in Salinas Pueblo Missions National Monument

Land cover type	Species	Common name	Cover (%)	Frequency (%)
Grassland	*Convolvulus arvensis*	field bindweed	9.379	25.00
	Kochia scoparia	common kochia	7.967	58.33
	Poa pratensis	Kentucky bluegrass	0.050	25.00
	Salsola tragus	prickly Russian thistle	0.046	25.00
	Lactuca serriola	wild lettuce	0.042	8.33
	Taraxacum officinale	common dandelion	0.004	8.33
	Bromus japonicus	Japanese brome	0.004	8.33
	Erodium cicutarium	redstem stork's bill	0	25.00
	Tragopogon dubius	Western goat's beard	0	16.67
	Ulmus pumila	Siberian elm	0	16.67
	Tamarix spp.	tamarisk	0	8.33
	Melilotus officinalis	yellow sweetclover	0	8.33
	Bromus tectorum	cheat grass	0	8.33
	Rumex crispus	curly dock	0	8.33
	Marrubium vulgare	horehound	0	8.33
	Eleusine indica	goose grass	0	8.33
	Malus pumila	apple tree	0	8.33
PJ Woodland	*Marrubium vulgare*	horehound	0.013	2.56
	Salsola tragus	prickly Russian thistle	0.001	2.56
	Rumex crispus	curly dock	0	2.56
	Melilotus officinalis	yellow sweetclover	0	2.56
	Medicago lupulina	black medic	0	2.56
	Taraxacum officinale	common dandelion	0	2.56
	Kochia scoparia	common kochia	0	2.56
	Erodium cicutarium	redstem stork's bill	0	2.56
	Bromus tectorum	cheat grass	0	2.56
	Malva neglecta	cheeseweed	0	2.56
	Bromus japonicus	Japanese brome	0	2.56
PJ Woodland & Savanna	*Salsola tragus*	prickly Russian thistle	0.003	8.33
	Convolvulus arvensis	field bindweed	0.001	1.67
	Kochia scoparia	common kochia	0.001	3.33
	Marrubium vulgare	horehound	0.001	5.00
	Carduus nutans	nodding plumeless thistle	0	1.67
	Melilotus officinalis	yellow sweetclover	0	1.67
	Rumex crispus	curly dock	0	1.67
	Tamarix spp.	tamarisk	0	1.67
	Taraxacum officinale	common dandelion	0	1.67
	Tragopogon dubius	western goat's beard	0	1.67
	Ulmus pumila	Siberian elm	0	1.67
Riparian	*Convolvulus arvensis*	field bindweed	15.017	100.00
	Melilotus officinalis	yellow sweetclover	0.867	100.00
	Rumex crispus	curly dock	0.833	33.33

Table 4, continued. Average percent cover for exotic plant species by land use type in Salinas Pueblo Missions National Monument

Park unit	Species	Common name	Cover (%)	Frequency (%)
	Bromus catharticus	rescue brome	0.333	66.67
	Poa pratensis	Kentucky bluegrass	0.183	66.67
	Bromus tectorum	cheat grass	0.167	33.33
	Sisymbrium altissimum	tumble mustard	0.017	33.33
	Tragopogon dubius	western goat's beard	0.017	66.67
	Erodium cicutarium	redstem stork's bill	0.017	66.67
	Taraxacum officinale	common dandelion	0.017	33.33
	Tamarix spp.	tamarisk	0	33.33
	Kochia scoparia	common kochia	0	33.33
	Marrubium vulgare	horehound	0	33.33
Riparian Shrubland	*Marrubium vulgare*	horehound	0.050	100.00
	Tamarix spp.	tamarisk	0	100.00
	Rumex crispus	curly dock	0	100.00
	Melilotus officinalis	yellow sweetclover	0	100.00
	Bromus catharticus	rescue brome	0	100.00
Shrubland	*Marrubium vulgare*	horehound	9.010	100.00
Urban	*Marrubium vulgare*	horehound	0.025	50.00

4). The Shrubland land cover type had the third highest average exotic plant cover with 9.01% (fig. 6), all of which was *Marrubium vulgare* (table 4). The Riparian Shrubland land cover type had the fourth highest average exotic plant cover with 0.05% (fig. 6), all of which was *Marrubium vulgare*. The Urban land cover type had the fifth average exotic plant cover with 0.025%, all of which was *Marrubium vulgare*. The Pinyon-Juniper Woodland land cover type had the sixth highest average exotic plant cover with 0.01% (fig. 6). The Pinyon-Juniper Woodland and Savanna land cover type had the seventh highest average exotic plant cover with 0.006% (fig. 6). No exotic species were recorded within the belt transects of the Sparsely Vegetated land cover type. For a map of the percent cover of exotics on each transect with land cover types, see figure 7.

Number of exotics

We found a total of 15 exotic species within the 125 belt transects and 18 exotic species within the 125 grid cells (fig. 8; appendix B). On average there were 0.39 exotic species for each transect and 0.75 exotic species within every grid cell throughout the park (fig. 9). These numbers were so low because 90 out of the 125 grid cells (72%) did not have any exotic species present. The average number of exotic species within various park units was 1.3 species in the Abo units, 0.1 species in the Gran Quivira units, and 3.2 species within the Quarai units (fig. 10). The average number of exotic species within the land cover types is as follows: 7 species in the Riparian land cover type, 5 species in the Riparain Shrubland cover type, 2.8 species in the Grassland cover type, 1 species in the Shrubland land cover type, 0.5 species in the Urban land cover type, 0.3 species in the Pinyon-Juniper Woodland and Savanna land cover type, and 0.28 species in the Pinyon-Juniper Woodland land cover type (fig. 11).

We collected five species as voucher specimens because they were new species within the monument boundary. The five species were *Ailanthus altissima* (tree of heaven), *Bromus japonicus* (Japanese brome), *Eleusine indica* (goose grass), *Kochia scoparia*, and *Malus pumila* (apple). *Ailanthus altissima* was found within the monument but not within

DAVE POWELL / USDA FOREST SERVICE

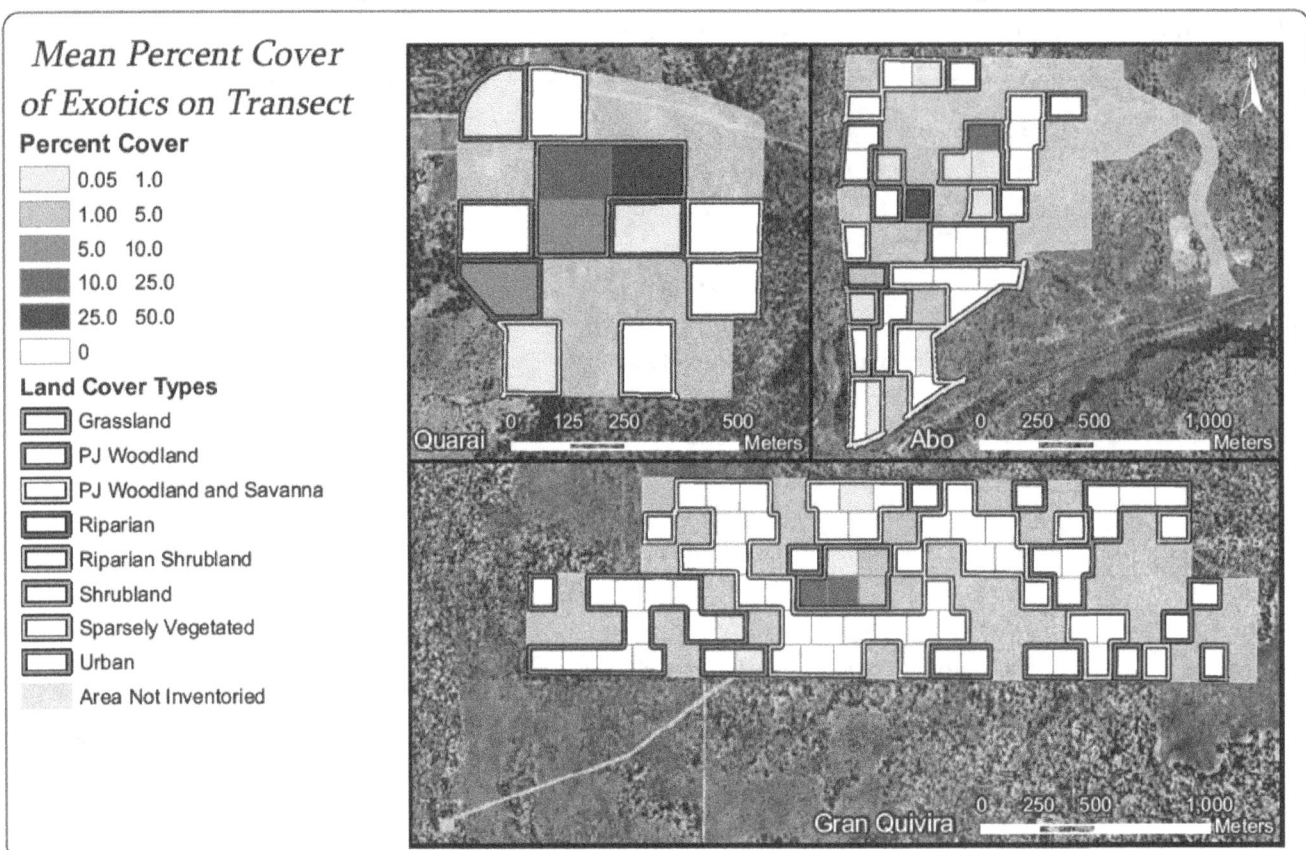

Mean Percent Cover of Exotics on Transect

Percent Cover

	0.05 1.0
	1.00 5.0
	5.0 10.0
	10.0 25.0
	25.0 50.0
	0

Land Cover Types

- Grassland
- PJ Woodland
- PJ Woodland and Savanna
- Riparian
- Riparian Shrubland
- Shrubland
- Sparsely Vegetated
- Urban
- Area Not Inventoried

Figure 7. Mean percent cover for exotic plants by grid cell and land cover type using 50-m belt transect data. Grassland belt transects were three meters in width (150 m²), the Pinyon-Juniper Woodland and Savanna belt transects were four meters in width (200 m²) and all other land cover type belt transects were seven meters in width (350 m²). The total area sampled was 25,800 m², approximately 3 ha. We calculated the percent exotic cover by calculating a midpoint for each cover class and then calculating the mean from the midpoint data (N=125).

in any of the grid cells. *Bromus japonicus* was found in one belt transect in grid cell 192 within the Quarai park unit and Grassland land type. *Bromus japonicus* was also found off transect in grid cell 183 in the Quarai park unit and PJ Woodland land type. *Kochia scoparia* was found in seven belt transects; it was found in grid cell 3 in the Abo park unit in the Pinyon-Juniper Woodland and Savanna land cover type and in grid cells 20, 25, 26, and 39 within the Abo park unit in the Grassland land cover type and in grid cells 187 and 188 in the Quarai park unit and Grassland land type. *Kochia scoparia* was also found off transect in grid cell 46 in the Abo park uni in the PJ Woodland land cover type, grid cell 61 in the Abo park unit and PJ Woodland and Savanna land cover type, in grid cell 191 in the Quarai park unit and Riparian land cover type and in grid cell 192 in the Quarai park unit and Grassland land cover type. *Eleusine indica* was found in grid cell 26 within the Abo park unit in the Grassland cover type. *Malus pumila* was found in grid cell 187 within the Quarai park

unit and Grassland cover type. For a map of the number of exotic species per grid cell and land cover types, see figure 12).

Number of exotics by park unit

The Quarai park unit had the highest average number (3.2) of exotic species within the grid cells (fig. 9). The Abo park unit had the next highest average number (1.3) of exotic species within their respective grid cells followed by the Gran Quivira park unit with less than one (0.13) species within the Gran Quivira grid cells (fig. 9). Grid cells 192 in the Quarai unit and 50 in the Abo unit had the highest number of exotic species with 10 in each, followed by 8 exotic species in grid cell 26 in the Abo unit, 6 exotic species in grid cell 191 (Quarai), 5 exotic species in grid cells 197, 193, and 187 (all in Quarai) as well as 5 in grid cell 53 (Abo) (table 3).The Gran Quivira park unit had the highest number (67) of grid cells with no exotic species, followed by the Abo park unit (19) and the Quarai park unit (4) (table 3).

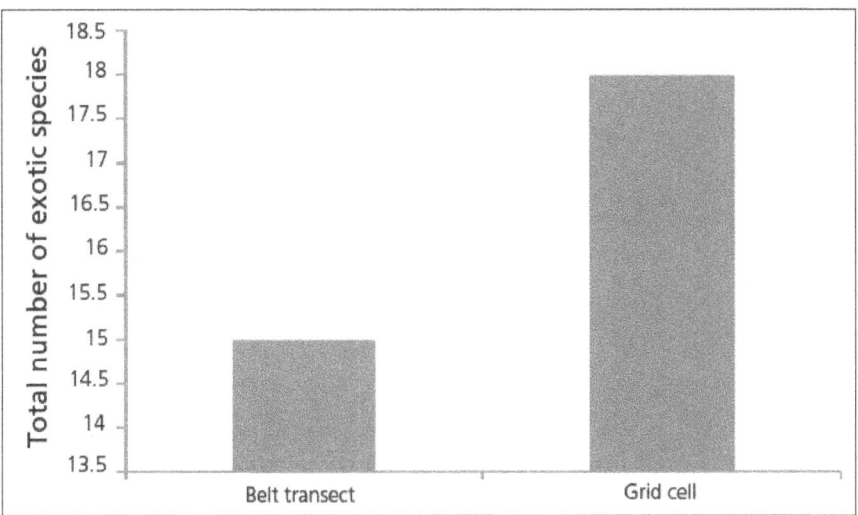

Figure 8. Total number of exotic species in Salinas Pueblo Missions National Monument found in 50-m belt transects and grid cells, approximately 2 ha each (N=125). Grassland belt transects were three meters in width (150 m²), the Pinyon-Juniper Woodland and Savanna belt transects were four meters in width (200 m²) and all other land cover type belt transects were seven meters in width (350 m²).

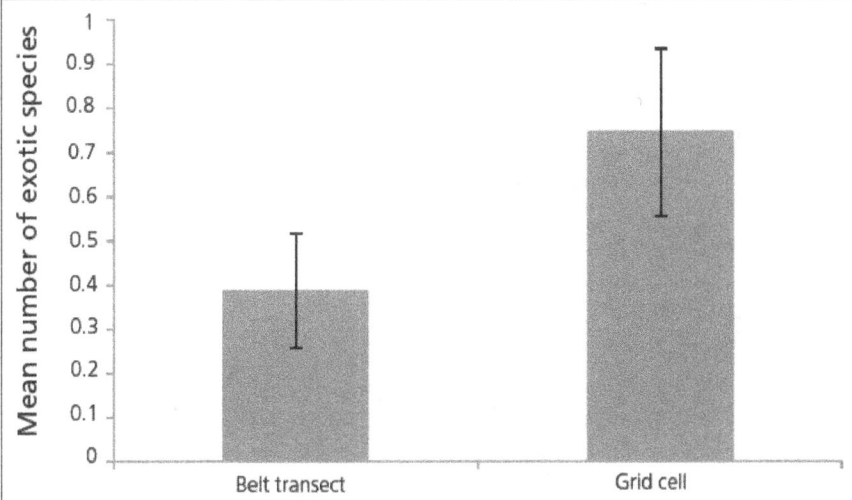

Figure 9. Mean number of exotic species in Salinas Pueblo Missions National Monument found in 50-m belt transects and grid cells, approximately 2 ha each (N=125). Grassland belt transects were three meters in width (150 m²), the Pinyon-Juniper Woodland and Savanna belt transects were four meters in width (200 m²) and all other land cover type belt transects were seven meters in width (350 m²). Error bars represent ±SEM.

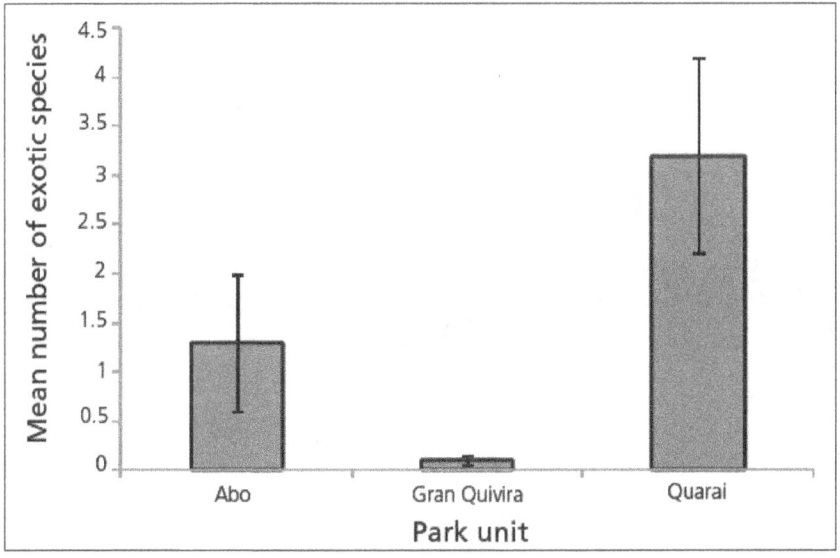

Figure 10. Mean number of exotic species by park unit in Salinas Pueblo Missions National Monument using grid cell data, approximately 2 ha each (N=125). We calculated the mean number of exotic species by dividing the total number of species within a grid cell by the number of grid cells for each park unit. Error bars represent ±SEM.

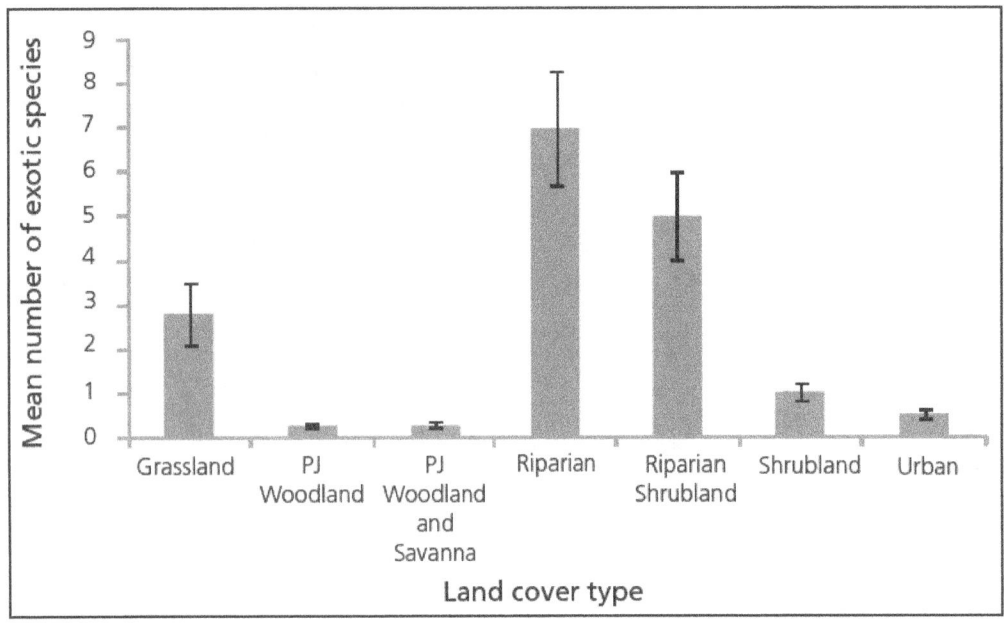

Figure 11. Mean number of exotic species by land cover type in Salinas Pueblo Missions National Monument using grid cell data, approximately 2 ha each (N=125). We calculated the mean number of exotic species by dividing the total number of species within a land cover type in a grid cell by the number of grid cells for each land cover type. There were no exotic species present in the Sparsely Vegetated land cover type grid cells. Error bars represent ±SEM.

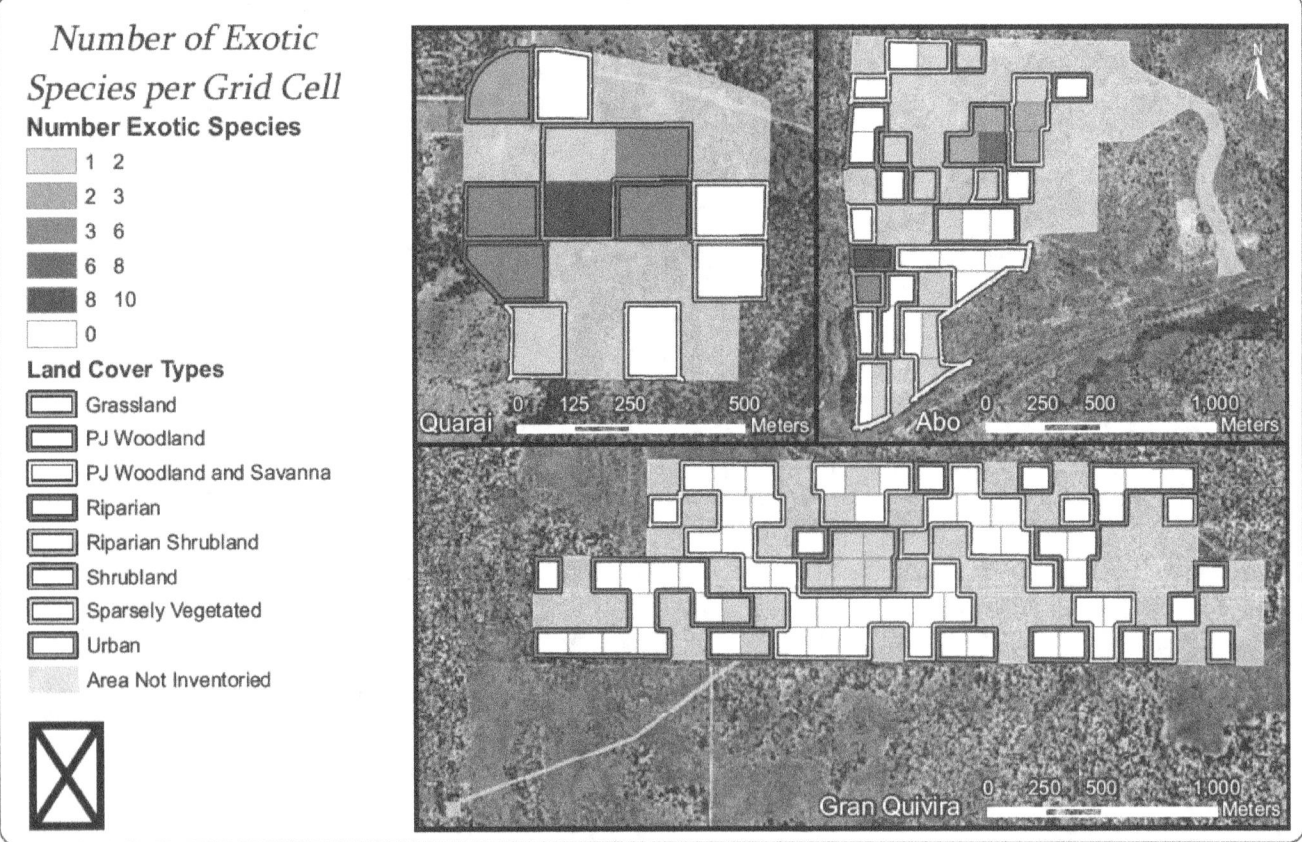

Figure 12. Number of exotic species in grid cells. Each grid cell was approximately two ha each. We identified eight land cover types: Grassland (12 grid cells), Pinyon-Juniper Woodland (39 grid cells), Pinyon-Juniper Woodland and Savanna (60 grid cells), Riparian (3 grid cells), Riparian Shrubland (1 grid cell), Shrubland (5 grid cells), Sparsely Vegetated (3 grid cells), and Urban (2 grid cells).

Number of exotics by land cover type

The Riparian land cover type had the highest average number of exotic species for the grid cells (7), followed by the Riparian Shrubland land cover type (5), Grassland (2.8), Shrubland (1), Urban (0.5), Pinyon-Juniper Woodland and Savanna (0.3), and Pinyon-Juniper Woodland (0.3) (fig. 11). Grid cell 192 in the Grassland land cover type and 50 in the Riparian land cover type had the highest number of exotic species with 10, followed by 8 exotic species in grid cell 26 in Grassland land cover type, 6 exotic species in grid cell 191 (Riparian) and 5 exotic species in each of grid cells 197 (Riparian), 193 (Pinyon-Juniper Woodland), 187 (Grassland) and 53 (Riparian Shrubland) (table 4). The Pinyon-Juniper Woodland Savanna had the highest number of grid cells (48) with no exotic species present followed by the Pinyon-Juniper Woodland land cover type with 34, the Grassland land cover type with four grid cells, the Sparsely Vegetated land cover type with three grid cells, and the Urban land cover types with one grid cell (appendix A).

Frequency

Frequency by park unit

Four exotic species had frequency values of 10 or higher in the Abo park unit (table 3). Only one exotic species was found in the Gran Quivira park unit: *Marrubium vulgare* had a frequency of 12.99 (table 3). Seven exotic species had frequency values of 25 or higher in the Quarai park unit, meaning that these individual species were found in more than a quarter (3) of the 12 Quarai park unit grid cells (table 3). *Convolvulus arvensis* had the highest frequency with 41.67, followed by *Kochia scoparia* with 33.33, and *Bromus tectorum, Erodium cicutarium, Poa pratensis, Salsola tragus,* and *Tragopogon dubius* with 25.00 frequency values (table 3).

Frequency by land cover type

Five exotic species had frequency values of 25 or higher in the Grassland land cover type, meaning that these individual species were found in more than a quarter (3) of the 12 Grassland grid cells (table 4). *Kochia scoparia* had the highest frequency with 58.33

followed by *Convolvulus arvensis, Erodium cicutarium, Poa pratensis,* and *Salsola tragus* all with 25 (table 4). No exotic species had a frequency value of 10 or higher in the Pinyon-Juniper Woodland land cover type. Two exotic species had frequency values of 100 in the Riparian land cover type, meaning that these individual species were found in all three of the Riparian grid cells (table 4). *Convolvulus arvensis* and *Melilotus officinalis* both had frequency values of 100 (table 4). Five species were found in the Riparian Shrubland grid cells. All five species had frequency values of 100, meaning that they were found in the one grid cell classified as Riparian Shrubland. One exotic species was found in the Shrubland land cover type: *Marrubium vulgare* had a frequency of 100 (table 4). There were no exotic species found in the Sparsely Vegetated land cover type. Only one species was found in the Urban land cover type. *Marrubium vulgare* was found in one of the two Urban grid cells and had a frequency value of 50 (table 4).

Environmental variables

We calculated environmental variables along the 125 belt transects. The average aspect was 210,° or a south/southwest aspect. The average slope was 0.59%. The average percent rock was 17.3% and average percent bare soil was 30.2%. Average soil disturbance was categorized as having light to no disturbance, where light disturbance is classified as having less than 40% of organic soil removed. Average tree canopy cover was 24.9% (table 5).

Environmental variables by park unit

All environmental variables differed by park unit (table 5). Average aspect ranged from 163°, or south/southeasterly aspect, for the Abo unit, to 236°, or south/southwesterly aspect, for the Gran Quivira unit. Average slope ranged from a negative slope of 5.6% in the Quarai unit to a positive slope of 2.16% in the Gran Quivira unit. Average percent rock ranged 40% in the Abo unit to 7.7% in the Gran Quivira unit. In contrast, average cover of bare soil was 34.9% at Gran Quivira and 22% at Abo and Quarai (table 5). Soil disturbance varied only slightly, but not significantly, among the three park units,

Table 5. Environmental variable averages for Salinas Pueblo Missions National Monument by park unit.

Park unit	Aspect (°)	Slope (%)	Rock (%)	Bare soil (%)	Soil disturbance	Tree canopy cover (%)
Abo	163	-1.15	40.0	22.8	4.92	8.7
Gran Quivira	236	2.16	7.7	34.9	4.80	32.9
Quarai	178	-5.60	10.8	22.5	4.78	21.6
Entire park	210	0.59	17.3	30.2	4.84	24.9

Note: We used the following soil disturbance scale: 1=bladed road, 2=heavy disturbance where more than 75% of the organic soil had been removed, 3=intermediate disturbance where 40-75% of the organic soil has been removed, 4=light disturbance where less than 45% of organic soil has been removed, and 5=there is no disturbance (Korb et al. 2007).

Table 6. Environmental variable averages for Salinas Pueblo Missions National Monument by land cover type.

Land use type	Aspect (°)	Slope (%)	Rock (%)	Bare soil (%)	Soil disturbance	Tree canopy cover (%)
Grassland	142	0.18	10.8	25.0	4.92	5.0
Pinyon-Juniper Woodland	224	1.25	16.6	34.2	4.81	35.8
Pinyon-Juniper Woodland and Savanna	220	0.15	17.2	32.0	4.86	23.2
Riparian	174	-0.67	6.7	10.0	4.66	13.3
Riparian Shrubland	34	-1.00	30.0	10.0	4.70	20.0
Shrubland	183	0	22.0	10.0	4.90	10.0
Sparsely Vegetated	213	0	63.3	13.3	4.90	23.3
Urban	221	9.00	0	50.0	4.30	50.0

Note: We used the following soil disturbance scale: 1=bladed road, 2=heavy disturbance where more than 75% of the organic soil had been removed, 3=intermediate disturbance where 40-75% of the organic soil has been removed, 4=light disturbance where less than 45% of organic soil has been removed, and 5=there is no disturbance (Korb et al. 2007)

with Quarai having slightly higher soil disturbance (4.78) than at Abo, which had virtually no soil disturbance (4.92). Tree canopy cover was highest within the Gran Quivira site (32.8%) and lowest within the Abo unit (8.7%).

Environmental variables by land cover type

All environmental variables differed by land cover type (table 6). Average aspect ranged from 34°, or north/northeasterly aspect, in the Riparian Shrubland to 224°, or south/southwesterly aspect, in the Pinyon-Juniper Woodland land cover type. Average slope ranged from a positive slope of 9% in the Urban land cover type to a negative slope of 1% in the Riparian Shrubland land cover type. Average percent rock ranged from 63.3% in the Sparsely Vegetated land cover

type to 0% in the Urban land cover type. In contrast, average cover of bare soil was 50% for the Urban land cover type and 10% for the Riparian, Riparian Shrubland, and Shrubland land cover types (table 6). Average soil disturbance varied only slightly among the land cover types, ranging from 4.3 in the urban land cover type to 4.92 in the Grassland land cover type. A value of 4 represents light disturbance where less than 45% of organic soil has been removed, and a value of 5 represents no disturbance (table 6). Tree canopy cover was highest in the Pinyon-Juniper Woodland land cover type (35.8%) and lowest within the Grassland land cover type (5%).

Discussion

Class A species

The New Mexico Department of Agriculture has listed 37 species as noxious weeds for control and eradication in accordance with the Noxious Weed Management Act of 1998 (Office of the Director/Secretary 1998). The New Mexico Department of Agriculture updated this list in April 2009 to include a new list of watch list species. Government officials have divided New Mexico's noxious weed list into four categories. Class A species have the highest priority because they currently are not found or are limited in distribution in New Mexico. We found no Class A noxious species in the park.

Class B species

We found one species in the monument that is classified as a Class B exotic species in New Mexico: *Carduus nutans* (musk thistle) (fig. 13). Class B species are species limited to portions of the state whose infestations should be contained to prevent further spread. We found *Carduus nutans* in only one grid cell in the Abo park unit and the Pinyon-Juniper Woodland and Savanna land cover type (appendix C).

Carduus nutans is a biennial forb that reproduces from seed and is allelopathic, preventing germination and growth of adjacent species and stimulating recruitment of its own seedlings (Wardle et al. 1993). *Carduus nutans* can grow in dense stands in disturbed areas or overgrazed pastures. An individual plant of *Carduus nutans* can produce up to 10,000 seeds that can remain viable for up to 15 years in the seedbank (Desrochers et al. 1988). Seeds are its only means of reproduction. A combination of mechanical, chemical, and biological control methods can eradicate *Carduus nutans*. Land managers can most effectively remove *Carduus nutans* mechanically by removal of rosettes before plants bolt and chemically by treatment with herbicide application (McCarty and Hatting 1975). Biological control agents include weevils, *Cheilosa corydon* (thistle crown fly) and *Puccinia carduorum* (musk thistle rust) (Rees et al. 1996).

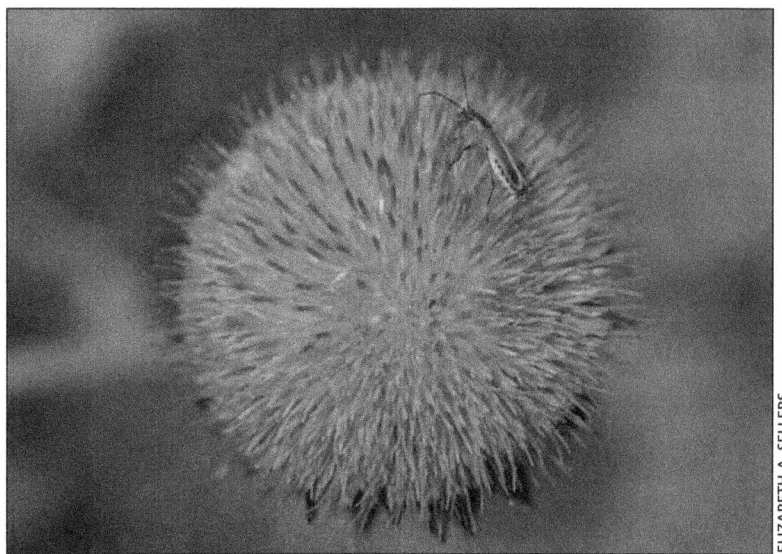

ELIZABETH A. SELLERS

Figure 13. *Carduus nutans* is a Class B species—species limited to portions of the state and whose infestations should be contained to prevent further spread.

Class C species

We found three of the six Class C exotic species listed by the New Mexico Department of Agriculture: *Bromus tectorum*, *Tamarix* spp., and *Ulmus pumila*. Class C species are widespread in New Mexico and their treatment should be decided by land managers at the local level, based on control feasibility and the degree of infestation.

Bromus tectorum

The only belt transect that had *Bromus tectorum* (fig. 14) was in grid cell 197 with 0.5% cover. This grid cell is in the Quarai park unit and classified as the Riparian land cover type. *Bromus tectorum* was in 25% of all the Quarai grid cells: grid cell 192 (Grassland land cover type), grid cell 193 (Pinyon-Juniper Woodland land cover type), and grid cell 197 (Riparian land cover type) (appendix A).

Bromus tectorum is a winter annual grass that can rapidly grow in spring because it can germinate at low temperatures. This rapid growth allows it to compete with native vegetation in cold, semi-arid environments (Harris 1967). An individual plant of *Bromus tectorum* can produce up to 5,000 seeds under optimal conditions (Young et al. 1987). *Bromus tectorum* seeds germinate fast and have high success rates under a variety of conditions, but they can also delay germina-

Figure 14. *Bromus tectorum* is a Class C species—species that are widespread in New Mexico and whose threatment should be decided on by local land managers.

CHRIS EVANS

Figure 15. *Tamarix* spp. was present in 11% of the grid cells in the Abo unit.

STEVE DEWEY

Figure 16. *Ulmus pumila* was found in three of the grid cells.

JOHN M. RANDALL

tion for up to two or three years (Goodwin et al. 1996). Disturbance—especially livestock grazing, tree removal, and fire—allows *Bromus tectorum* to flourish from seeds from extant plants or the seedbank. But *Bromus tectorum* can also establish in small openings in relatively undisturbed native vegetation (Hulbert 1955). *Bromus tectorum* invasions may result in a self-perpetuating grass-fire cycle. The cycle depends on vegetation, environmental, and fire conditions, but it generally results in *Bromus tectorum* outcompeting native vegetation and forming a monoculture that allows the dried plants to burn readily in spring and fall. These burns create microsites for new *Bromus tectorum* plants to establish, which creates a fine fuelbed that increases fire frequency and intensity (Young and Evans 1978). Once *Bromus tectorum* is well-established, eradicating it is extremely difficult and can create its own steady-state; therefore efforts to control *Bromus tectorum* should be taken when abundance is low. Control methods for *Bromus tectorum* must include multiple methods over successive years, including physical and mechanical removal, herbicide use, grazing, fire with appropriate timing, and seeding and transplants of native perennials (Mosely et al. 1999).

Tamarix spp.

Tamarix spp. (fig. 15) was not present in any of the belt transects but was present in approximately 11% of all grid cells within the Abo park unit (table 3): grid cell 21 (Pinyon-Juniper Woodland and Savanna land cover type), 26 (Grassland land cover type), 50 (Riparian land cover type), and 53 (Riparian Shrubland land cover type) (table 4).

Tamarix chinensis is an aggressive exotic tree that negatively impacts native plant composition and regeneration of (*Populus* spp.) cottonwoods and *Salix* spp. (willows) in arid, southwestern riparian environments. It may also alter stream hydrology (Carman and Brotherson 1982; Howe and Knoff 1991; Sala et al. 1996). *Tamarix chinensis* needs integrated management for successful eradication including removal of aboveground foliage and stems through cutting or burning and the application of herbicide to stumps, also known as the cut-stump method (Chavez 1996; Caplin 2002).

Ulmus pumila

Ulmus pumila (fig. 16) was not found in any of the belt transects but was found in two grid cells in the Abo park unit: grid cell 26 (Grassland land cover type) and grid cell 27 (Pinyon-Juniper Woodland and Savanna land cover type). Its frequency in the Abo park unit was 8%. In addition, it was found in one grid cell (192) in the Quarai park unit in the Grassland land cover type (appendix A).

Species with the highest cover

Convolvulus arvensis

Convolvulus arvensis (field bindweed) (fig. 17) had the highest plant cover (1.26%) within the entire monument, with a frequency of approximately 5.5% in the Abo park unit and 42% in the Quarai park unit (table 3). *Convolvulus arvensis* was found in the Grassland, PJ Woodland and Savanna, and Riparian land cover types. Field bindweed is an exotic species that thrives in agricultural areas, disturbed areas, or in moist riparian or irrigated areas. Field bindweed is a perennial vine that has deep, persistent, spreading roots. Field bindweed taproots can by anywhere between 2 to 10 feet (0.5-3 m) or more long. Lateral roots are found primarily in the top 12 inches (30 cm) of soil (Zouhar 2004). The primary mode of regeneration is through rhizomes. Old roots that have been cut off successively for several years are capable of producing a thousand or more slender rhizomes from the severed end and give rise to a leafy growth above ground (Kennedy and Crafts 1931). Field bindweed seeds remain viable in the soil seed bank for approximately 20 to 50 years. Field bindweed control strategies need to include seedbank reduction, prevention of seedling growth, depleting food reserves in the root systems, and preventing the land disturbance that promotes its spread (Zouhar 2004). Biocontrol and herbicide applications are also options for controlling field bindweed.

Kochia scoparia

Kochia scoparia (fig. 18) had the second highest plant cover (0.77%) within the entire monument, with a frequency of approximately 19% in the Abo park unit and 33%

Figure 17. *Convolvulus arvensis* had the highest plant cover in the monument.

K. GEORGE BECK AND JAMES SEBASTIAN

PHIL WESTRA

Figure 18. *Kochia scoparia* had the second highest average plant cover in the monument Abo unit.

in the Quarai park unit (table 3). *Kochia scoparia* was found within the Grassland, Pinyon-Juniper Woodland, Pinyon-Juniper Woodland and Savanna, and Riparian land cover types (table 4). *Kochia scoparia* had the highest overall exotic plant cover (2.1%) in the Abo unit and second highest in the Quarai park unit (table 3). The highest percent cover of *Kochia scoparia* was in grid cells 20 and 39 with 37.5% cover. Research in eastern Colorado along the Arkansas River

Figure 19. *Ailanthus altissima* had not been documented in the monument before this inventory.

per year, on average (Eberlein and Fore 1984). Kochia seeds remain viable for less than one year and have a dormancy period of two or three months, germinating in early spring through summer (Iverson and Wali 1982). Kochia seeds are primarily dispersed through stem abscission, hence the common name "tumbleweed", but also via wind and water. *Kochia scoparia* can be effectively controlled with numerous herbicides (Thomas and Donaghy 1991). Renz (2008) recommends a combination of herbicide, grazing, and mechanical treatments to eradicate *Kochia scoparia* in New Mexico. Fire immediately kills *Kochia scoparia*, but it is unknown whether fire destroys the seedbank.

Conclusion

We found low (2.5%) exotic weed cover overall and a moderate number (18) of exotic plants in the grid cells surveyed at Salinas Pueblo Missions National Monument. The results from this study will allow land managers to target specific exotic species that the New Mexico Department of Agriculture has listed as noxious weeds for control and eradication, in accordance with the Noxious Weed Management Act of 1998 (Office of the Director/Secretary 1998). In addition, land managers should target the five new occurrences of exotic plant species within the monument (*Ailanthus altissima* (fig. 19), *Bromus japonicus* (fig. 20), *Eleusine indica* (fig. 21), *Kochia scoparia*, and *Malus pumila*) before they spread to new areas and become established. Finally, land managers should identify and control exotic species with high cover (abundance) and/or high frequency (spatial distribution). Also exotic weed control efforts should focus on the Abo and Quarai park units because they had significantly higher percentages of exotic cover and frequencies than the Gran Quivira park unit, which has low exotic cover and few exotic species. Finally, exotic weed control efforts should focus on the Riparian, Grassland, and Shrubland land cover types, which had significantly higher percentages of exotic cover and frequencies than the other land cover types within the monument.

The best method to manage these exotic species is to prevent their further establishment

has shown that *Kochia scoparia* can form a monoculture under riparian vegetation dominated by *Tamarix* spp. (Lindauer 1983), indicating that *Kochia scoparia* has the potential to increase in abundance in riparian areas of the monument.

Kochia scoparia is an annual forb that farmers in dry areas commonly use as a drought-resistant forage crop because of its low water requirements and resistance to diseases and insects (Eberlein and Fore 1984). *Kochia scoparia* plants are allelopathic, allowing it to inhibit growth of adjacent plants and rapidly colonize disturbed areas (Lodhi 1979). An individual plant can produce 14,600 seeds

JOHN M. RANDALL

Figure 20. *Bromus japonicus* was first found in the monument during this inventory.

JOHN D. BYRD

Figure 21. *Eleusine indica* is one of the exotic species newly documented within the monument.

and spread through avoiding management actions that encourage invasion, maintaining healthy native plant communities, and monitoring for the presence of exotic species each year (Sheley et al. 1999). To restore native plants to areas with exotic vegetation, research has shown that the soil must be manipulated, specifically by changing mycorrhizal fungal abundance, soil pathogens, and slowing nutrient cycling rates (Kulmatiski et al. 2006). Land managers should continue monitoring to quantify new exotic species occurrences and changes in abundance and frequency of existing exotic species.

No one optimum method exists for controlling and eradicating all exotic species; therefore, land managers will be required to utilize an integrated approach of mechanical, biological, cultural, and chemical treatments for the individual species being targeted for removal and for the site specific vegetation, environmental, and cultural conditions. Dispersal of the exotic propagule pool will need to be minimized during exotic weed

treatment (Krueger-Mangold et al. 2006). Native species will need to be promoted through a variety of methods, including seeding, plugging, transplants, and natural reestablishment from in situ native vegetation (Albrecht et al. 2005). A successional management approach that incorporates ecological processes (plant succession) and a long-term perspective on controlling exotic species is paramount for the long-term success of establishing native plant communities (Krueger-Mangold et al. 2006). The establishment of self-sustaining native plant communities is one of the most effective methods to prevent future exotic plant invasions and should be the ultimate goal of any restoration efforts to remove exotic species. Numerous studies in a variety of plant communities have shown site specific examples where seeding, transplanting of native species, or in situ native species competition can suppress exotic plant species (Cox and Anderson 2004, Talluto et al. 2006, Endress et al. 2008, Getz and Baker 2008, Reinhardt Adamsand Galatowitsch 2008, Rowe and Brown 2008).

Literature Cited

Albrecht, W. D., J. Maschinski, A. Mracna, and S. Murray. 2005. A community participatory project to restore a native grassland. Natural Areas Journal 25: 137-146.

Brooks, M. L., and D. A. Pyke. 2001. Invasive plants and fire in the deserts of North America. Pages 1–14 *in* K. E. M. Galley and T. P. Wilson, editors. Proceedings of the Invasive Species Workshop: the Role of Fire in the Control and Spread of Invasive Species. Fire Conference 2000: the First National Congress on Fire Ecology, Prevention, and Management. Miscellaneous Publication No. 11, Tall Timbers Research Station, Tallahassee, FL.

Brooks, T. M., R. A. Mittermeier, C. G. Mittermeier, G. A. B. Fonseca, A. B. Rylands, W. R. Konstant, P. Flick, J. Pilgrim, S. Oldfield, G. Magin, and C. Hilton-Taylor. 2002. Habitat loss and extinction in the hotspots of biodiversity. Conservation Biology 16: 909–923.

Caplan, T. 2002. Controlling Russian olives within cottonwood gallery forests along the Middle Rio Grande floodplain (New Mexico). Ecological Restoration 20(2): 138-139.

Carman, J. G., and J. D. Brotherson. 1982. Comparisons of sites infested and not infested with saltcedar (*Tamarix ramosissima*) and Russian olive (*Eleagnus angustifolia*). Weed Science 30: 360-364.

Chavez, R. A. 1996. Integrated weed management: concept and practice. Pages 32-36 *in* J. DiTomaso and C. E. Bell, editors. Proceedings of the saltcedar management workshop, June 12, 1996, Rancho Mirage, CA. University of California Cooperative Extension Service, Holtville, CA.

Cox, R. D., and V. J. Anderson. 2004. Increasing native diversity of cheatgrass-dominated rangeland through assisted succession. Rangeland Ecology and Management 57: 203-210.

Desrochers, A. M., J. F. Bain, and S. I. Warwick. 1988. The biology of Canadian weeds. 89. *Carduus nutans* L. and *Carduus acanthoides* L. Canadian Journal of Plant Science 68: 1053-1068.

DeVeaux, J. S., and E. B. Shultz. 1985. Devleopment of buffalo gourd (*Cucurbita foetidissima*) as a semiaridland starch and oil crop. Economic Botany 39 (4): 454-472.

Eberlein, C. V., and Z. Q. Fore. 1984. Kochia biology. Weeds Today 15(3): 5-7.

Endress, B. A., C. G. Parks, B. J. Naylor, and S. R. Radosevich. 2008. Herbicide and native grass seeding effects on sulfur cinquefoil (*Potentilla recta*)-infested grasslands. Invasive Plant Science and Management 1: 50-58.

European and Mediterranean Plant Protection Organization. 2007. Data sheets on quarantine pests. *Solanum elaeagnifolium*. Bulletin OEPP/EPPO Bulletin 37: 236–245.

Getz, H. L., and W. L. Baker 2008. Initial invasion of cheatgrass (*Bromus tectorum*) into burned pinyon-juniper woodlands in western Colorado. The American Midland Naturalist 159: 489-497.

Goodwin, J. R., P. S. Doescher, and L. E. Eddleman. 1996. Germination of Idaho fescue and cheatgrass seeds from coexisting populations. Northwest Science 70(3): 230-241.

Harris, G. A. 1967. Some competitive relationships between *Agropyron spicatum* and *Bromus tectorum*. Ecological Monographs 37(2): 89-111.

Howe, W. H, and F. L. Knoff. 1991. On the imminent decline of Rio Grande cottonwoods in central New Mexico. The Southwestern Naturalist 36(2): 218-224.

Hulbert, L. C. 1955. Ecological studies of *Bromus tectorum* and other annual bromegrasses. Ecological Monographs 25(2): 181-213.

Iverson, L. R., and M. K. Wali. 1982. Buried, viable seeds and their relation to revegetation after surface mining. Journal of Range Management 35(5): 648-652.

Kennedy, P. B., and Crafts, A. S. 1931. The anatomy of *Convolvulus arvensis*, wild morning-glory or field bind-weed. Hilgardia. 5(18): 591-622.

Korb, J. E., Fulé, P. Z., and B. Gideon. 2007. Diff erent restoration thinning treatments affect level of soil disturbance in ponderosa pine forests of northern Arizona, USA. Ecological Restoration 25(1): 43-49.

Krueger-Mangold, J. M., R. L. Sheley, T. J. Svejcar. 2006. Toward ecologically-based invasive plant management on rangeland. Weed Science 54: 597-605.

Kulmatiski, A., K. H. Beard, and J. M. Stark. 2006. Soil history as a primary control on plant invasion in abandoned agricultural fields. Journal of Applied Ecology 43: 868-876.

Lindauer, I. E. 1983. A comparison of the plant communities of the South Platte and Arkansas River drainages in eastern Colorado. The Southwestern Naturalist 28(3): 249-259.

Lodhi, M. A. K. 1979. Germination and decreased growth of *Kochia scoparia* in relation to its autoallelopathy. Canadian Journal of Botany 10: 1083-1088.

McCarty, M. K. and J. L. Hatting. 1975. Effects of herbicides or mowing on musk thistle seed production. Weed Research 15: 363-367.

Mosely, J. C., S. C. Bunting, and M. E. Manoukian. 1999. Cheat-grass. Pages 175-188 *in* R. L. Sheley and J. K. Petroff, editors. Biology and management of noxious rangeland weeds. Oregon State University Press, Corvallis, OR.

National Park Service. 1984. General management plan. Salinas Pueblo Missions National Monument, New Mexico. National Park Service, Santa Fe, NM

National Park Service. 2006. Salinas Pueblo Missions National Monument Park Visitation Report 2005. Park Use Statistics Office, National Park Service. Available at: http://www2.nature.nps.gov/stats/.

Office of the Director/Secretary. 1998. New Mexico noxious weed list (20 October 2003). New Mexico Department of Agriculture. Available at: http://plants.usda.gov/java/noxComposite.

Pimentel, D., L. Lach, R. Zuniga, and D. Morrison. 2000. Environmental and economic costs of non-indigenous species in the United States. Bioscience 50: 53-65.

Pimentel, D., R. Zuniga, and D. Morrison. 2004. Update on the environmental and economic costs associated with alien-invasive species in the United States. Ecological Economics 52: 273-288.

Rees, N. E., J. L. Littlefield, W. L. Bruckart, and A. Baudoin. 1996. Musk thistle: *Carduus nutans* (group). in N. E. Rees, P. C. Quimby, Jr. and G. L. Piper, [and others], editors. Biological control of weeds in the West. Western Society of Weed Science, in cooperation with: U.S. Department of Agriculture, Agricultural Research Service, Montana Department of Agriculture, Montana State University, Bozeman, MT.

Reinhardt Adams, C., and S. M. Galatowitsch. 2008. The transition from invasive species control to native species promotion and its dependence on seed density thresholds. Applied Vegetation Science 11: 131-138.

Renz, M.J. 2008. Management and restoration of areas infested with Russian thistle and Kochia in southern New Mexico. New Mexico State University Unpublished report, Las Cruces, NM.

Rowe, H. I., and C. S. Brown. 2008. Native plant growth and seedling establishment in soils influenced by *Bromus tectorum*. Rangeland Ecology and Management 61: 630-639.

Sala, A., S. D. Smith, and D. A. Devitt. 1996. Water use by *Tamarix ramosissima* and associated phreatophytes in a Mojave Desert floodplain. Ecological Applications 6: 888-898.

Sheley, R. L., M. Manoukian, and G. Marks. 1999. Preventing noxious weed invasion. Pages 69-72 in R. L. Sheley and J. K. Petroff, editors. Biology and management of noxious rangeland weeds. Oregon State University

Press, Corvallis, OR.

Talluto, M. V., K. Nash Suding, and P. A. Bowler. 2006. Factors affecting understory establishment in coastal sage scrub restoration. Madroño 53: 55-59.

Thomas, A. G., and D. I. Donaghy. 1991. A survey of the occurrence of seedling weeds in spring annual crops in Manitoba. Canadian Journal of Plant Science 71(3): 811-820.

United States Department of the Interior. 2004. Environmental Assessment. For XTO energy to continue operating the Fee 9Y and the Fee 4-A natural gas wells. Salinas Pueblo Missions National Monument, New Mexico.

Wardle, D. A., K. S. Nicholson, and A. Rahman. 1993. Influence of plant age on the allelopathic potential of nodding thistle (*Carduus nutans* L.) against pasture grasses and legumes. Weed Research 33: 69-78.

Watson, A. K. 1980. The biology of Canadian weeds. 43. *Acroptilon* (*Centaurea*) *repens* (L.) DC. Canadian Journal of Plant Science 60: 993-1004.

Young, J. A., and R. A. Evans. 1978. Population dynamics after wildfires in sagebrush grasslands. Journal of Range Management 31(4): 283-289.

Young, J. A., R. A. Evans, R. E. Eckert, Jr., and K. L. Burgess. 1987. Cheatgrass. Rangelands 9(6): 266-270.

Young, C. C., J. L. Haack, L. W. Morrison, and M. D. DeBacker. 2007. Invasive exotic plant monitoring protocol for the Heartland Network Inventory and Monitoring Program. Natural Resource Report NPS/HTLN/NRR-2007/018. National Park Service, Fort Collins, CO.

Zouhar, K. 2004. *Convolvulus arvensis*. *in* Fire Effects Information System, U.S. Department of Agriculture, Forest Service, Rocky Mountain Research Station, Fire Sciences Laboratory. Available at: http://www.fs.fed.us/database/feis/ (accessed 3 December 2009).

Appendix A. Cover of Exotic Plant Species

Appendix A contains a list of exotic plant species with their percent covers for each grid cell by park unit and land cover type. Each grid cell was approximately two hectares. There are three park units at Salinas Pueblo Missions National Monument: Abo (36 grid cells), Gran Quivira (77 grid cells), and Quarai (12 grid cells). We identified land cover types by dominant species and physical land attributes. The eight land cover types were: Grassland (12 grid cells), Pinyon-Juniper Woodland (39 grid cells), Pinyon-Juniper Woodland and Savanna (60 grid cells), Riparian (3 grid cells), Riparian Shrubland (1 grid cell), Shrubland (5 grid cells), Sparsely Vegetated (3 grid cells), and Urban (2 grid cells). Grassland belt transects were three meters in width (150 m²), the Pinyon-Juniper Woodland and Savanna belt transects were in four meters in width (200 m²), and all other land cover type belt transects were seven meters in width (350 m²). We calculated the percent exotic cover for each species by calculating a midpoint for each cover class and then calculating the means from the midpoint data (N=125).

Grid cell	Park unit	Land cover type	Species	Cover (%)
3	Abo	PJ Woodland and Savanna	*Kochia scoparia*	0.05
20	Abo	Grassland	*Kochia scoparia*	37.50
20	Abo	Grassland	*Poa pratensis*	0.05
25	Abo	Grassland	*Kochia scoparia*	0.50
25	Abo	Grassland	*Salsola tragus*	0.50
26	Abo	Grassland	*Convolvulus arvensis*	0.05
26	Abo	Grassland	*Kochia scoparia*	0.05
26	Abo	Grassland	*Salsola tragus*	0.05
31	Abo	Grassland	*Poa pratensis*	0.05
33	Abo	PJ Woodland and Savanna	*Salsola tragus*	0.05
39	Abo	Grassland	*Kochia scoparia*	37.50
50	Abo	Riparian	*Convolvulus arvensis*	7.50
50	Abo	Riparian	*Rumex crispus*	2.50
50	Abo	Riparian	*Melilotus officinalis*	2.50
50	Abo	Riparian	*Bromus catharticus*	0.50
50	Abo	Riparian	*Sisymbrium altissimum*	0.05
50	Abo	Riparian	*Taraxacum officinale*	0.05
50	Abo	Riparian	*Erodium cicutarium*	0.05
53	Abo	Riparian Shrubland	*Marrubium vulgare*	0.05
59	Abo	PJ Woodland and Savanna	*Salsola tragus*	0.05
63	Abo	PJ Woodland and Savanna	*Salsola tragus*	0.05
71	Abo	PJ Woodland and Savanna	*Salsola tragus*	0.05
111	Gran Quivira	Shrubland	*Marrubium vulgare*	0.05
112	Gran Quivira	Shrubland	*Marrubium vulgare*	2.50
122	Gran Quivira	Shrubland	*Marrubium vulgare*	20.00
123	Gran Quivira	Shrubland	*Marrubium vulgare*	20.00
124	Gran Quivira	Shrubland	*Marrubium vulgare*	2.50
138	Gran Quivira	PJ Woodland	*Marrubium vulgare*	0.50
170	Gran Quivira	Urban	*Marrubium vulgare*	0.05
183	Quarai	PJ Woodland	*Salsola tragus*	0.05
187	Quarai	Grassland	*Convolvulus arvensis*	75.00
187	Quarai	Grassland	*Kochia scoparia*	0.05
188	Quarai	Grassland	*Kochia scoparia*	20.00
191	Quarai	Riparian	*Poa pratensis*	0.50
191	Quarai	Riparian	*Convolvulus arvensis*	0.05

Appendix A, continued.

Grid cell	Park unit	Land cover type	Species	Cover (%)
191	Quarai	Riparian	*Melilotus officinalis*	0.05
191	Quarai	Riparian	*Tragopogon dubius*	0.05
192	Quarai	Grassland	*Convolvulus arvensis*	37.50
192	Quarai	Grassland	*Poa pratensis*	0.50
192	Quarai	Grassland	*Lactuca serriola*	0.50
192	Quarai	Grassland	*Taraxacum officinale*	0.05
192	Quarai	Grassland	*Bromus japonicus*	0.05
197	Quarai	Riparian	*Convolvulus arvensis*	37.50
197	Quarai	Riparian	*Bromus catharticus*	0.50
197	Quarai	Riparian	*Bromus tectorum*	0.50
197	Quarai	Riparian	*Melilotus officinalis*	0.05
197	Quarai	Riparian	*Poa pratensis*	0.05
201	Quarai	PJ Woodland and Savanna	*Convolvulus arvensis*	0.05
201	Quarai	PJ Woodland and Savanna	*Salsola tragus*	0.05

Appendix B. Plant Species List

Appendix B is the plant species list by family for Salinas Pueblo Missions National Monument.

Family	Species	Common name
Agavaceae	*Yucca baccata*	banana yucca
	Yucca elata	soaptree yucca
	Yucca glauca	Great Plains yucca
Amaranthaceae	*Amaranthus retroflexus*	pigweed
	Tidestromia lanuginosa	honeymat
Anacardiaceae	*Rhus trilobata*	skunkbush sumac
Apiaceae	*Harbouria trachypleura*	whiskbroom parsley
Asclepiadaceae	*Asclepias asperula*	antelope horns
	Asclepias engelmanniana	Engelmann's milkweed
	Asclepias uncialis	wheel milkweed
Asteraceae	*Achillea millefolium*	bloodwort
	Artemisia campestris ssp. *caudata*	Pacific wormwood
	Artemisia carruthii	Carruth's sagebrush
	Artemisia filifolia	sand sagebush
	Artemisia tridentata	big sagebrush
	Berlandiera texana	Texas greeneyes
	Centaurea americana	American basketflower
	Chrysothamnus pulchellus	southwest rabbitbrush
	Cirsium neomexicanum	New Mexico thistle
	Cirsium ochrocentrum	yellowspine thistle
	Cirsium parryi	Parry's thistle
	Engelmannia peristenia	Engelmann's daisy
	Ericameria nauseosa	goldenbush
	Erigeron bellidiastrum var. *bellidiastrum*	western daisy fleabane
	Erigeron divergens	spreading daisy
	Gaillardia pulchella	Indian blanket
	Grindelia squarrosa	curleycup gumweed
	Gutierrezia microcephala	threadleaf snakeweed
	Gutierrezia sarothrae	broom snakeweed
	Heterosperma pinnatum	wingpetal
	Heterotheca villosa	hairy false goldaster
	Hymenopappus filifolius	cutleaf
	Hymenopappus flavescens var. *canotomentosus*	college flower
	Iva xanthifolia	burweed marshelder
	Lygodesmia grandiflora	largeflower skeletonplant
	Machaeranthera gracilis	slender goldenweed
	Machaeranthera pinnatifida	lacy tansy-aster
	Machaeranthera tanacetifolia	Takhoka-daisy
	Melampodium leucanthum	plains blackfoot
	Pectis angustifolia var. *angustifolia*	lemonscent
	Psilostrophe sparsiflora	greenstem paperflower

Appendix B, continued.		
Family	**Species**	**Common name**
	Psilostrophe tagetina var. *tagetina*	woolly paperflower
	Ratibida tagetes	green Mexican-hat
	Sanvitalia abertii	Albert creeping zinnia
	Senecio flaccidus var. *douglasii*	Douglas groundsel
	Senecio flaccidus var. *flaccidus*	threadleaf groundsel
	Sonchus arvensis	creeping sowthistle
	Symphyotrichum ascendens	western aster
	Symphyotrichum falcatum var. *commutatum*	white prairie aster
	Tetradymia canescens	gray horsebrush
	Tetraneuris acaulis var. *acaulis*	stemless actinea
	Tetraneuris argentea	perkysue
	Thelesperma filifolium var. *intermedium*	stiff greenthread
	Thelesperma megapotamicum	Hopi tea greenthread
	Townsendia annua	annual Townsend daisy
	Tragopogon dubius	Western goat's beard
	Verbesina encelioides	golden crownbeard
	Xanthium strumarium	cocklebur
	Zinnia grandiflora	RockyMountain zinnia
Berberidaceae	*Mahonia fremontii*	Fremont's mahonia
Boraginaceae	*Cryptantha angustifolia*	Panamint cryptantha
	Cryptantha cinerea var. *jamesii*	James' cryptantha
	Cryptantha crassisepala var. *elachantha*	thicksepal cryptantha
	Lappula occidentalis var. *occidentalis*	flatspine stickseed
	Lithospermum incisum	fringed gromwell
	Lithospermum multiflorum	manyflowered gromwell
Brassicaceae	*Arabis X divaricarpa*	spreading rockcress
	Descurainia sophia	flaxweed tansymustard
	Dimorphocarpa wislizeni	Wislizeni's spectaclepod
	Erysimum capitatum	coast wallflower
	Lepidium alyssoides var. *angustifolium*	mesa pepperwort
	Lepidium montanum	Montana pepperweed
	Lesquerella fendleri	Fendler bladderpod
	Lesquerella intermedia	Santa Fe bladderpod
	Rorippa sinuata	spreading yellowcress
	Schoenocrambe linearifolia	slimleaf plains mustard
	Sisymbrium altissimum	Jim Hill mustard
Cactaceae	*Escobaria vivipara* var. *vivipara*	pink pincushioncactus
	Opuntia erinacea	Mohave pricklypear cactus
	Opuntia imbricata	cholla
	Opuntia polyacantha	plains pricklypear
Chenopodiaceae	*Atriplex canescens*	fourwing saltbush
	Bassia hyssopifolia	fivehook bassia
	Chenopodium fremontii	Fremont goosefoot
	Chenopodium leptophyllum	narrowleaf goosefoot

Family	Species	Common name
	Chenopodium pratericola	desert goosefoot
	Krascheninnikovia lanata	winterfat
	Salsola tragus	prickly Russian thistle
Commelinaceae	*Tradescantia occidentalis*	prairie spiderwort
Convolvulaceae	*Convolvulus arvensis*	field bindweed
	Ipomoea leptophylla	bush morning-glory
Cucurbitaceae	*Cucurbita foetidissima*	Missouri gourd
Cupressaceae	*Juniperus monosperma*	oneseed juniper
	Carex occidentalis	western sedge
	Carex pellita	woolly sedge
	Carex praegracilis	clustered field sedge
	Cyperus schweinitzii	Schweinitz's flatsedge
	Eleocharis palustris	common spikerush
	Eleocharis parishii	Parish spikerush
	Eleocharis rostellata	beaked spike-rush
	Schoenoplectus americanus	American bulrush
	Schoenoplectus tabernaemontani	great bulrush
Elaeagnaceae	*Elaeagnus angustifolia*	Russian olive
Equisetaceae	*Equisetum arvense*	western horsetail
	Equisetum laevigatum	smooth horsetail
Euphorbiaceae	*Chamaesyce fendleri*	Fendler's sandmat
	Chamaesyce missurica	prairie sandmat
	Chamaesyce stictospora	slimseed sandmat
	Euphorbia davidii	David's spurge
Fabaceae	*Astragalus allochrous* var. *playanus*	Wooton's milkvetch
	Astragalus flexuosus	flexile milkvetch
	Astragalus praelongus var. *ellisiae*	Ellis' stinking milkvetch
	Caesalpinia drepanocarpa	sicklepod holdback
	Dalea cylindriceps	Andean prairieclover
	Dalea formosa	feather dalea
	Dalea nana	dwarf prairie clover
	Glycyrrhiza lepidota	American licorice
	Lupinus kingii	King's lupine
	Lupinus pusillus	rusty lupine
	Medicago lupulina	black medic
	Melilotus officinalis	yellow sweetclover
	Psoralidium lanceolatum	dune scurfpea
	Sophora nuttalliana	silky sophora
	Trifolium hybridum	alsike clover
Fagaceae	*Quercus emoryi*	Emory oak
	Quercus X pauciloba	wavyleaf oak
Fumariaceae	*Corydalis aurea*	golden corydalis
	Corydalis curvisiliqua ssp. *occidentalis*	curvepod fumewort
Geraniaceae	*Erodium cicutarium*	redstem stork's bill

Appendix B, continued.

Appendix B, continued.

Family	Species	Common name
	Geranium caespitosum var. *caespitosum*	pineywoods geranium
	Geranium caespitosum var. *eremophilum*	purple cluster geranium
	Geranium caespitosum var. *fremontii*	Fremont geranium
Grossulariaceae	*Ribes aureum*	golden currant
	Ribes cereum	wax currant
Hydrophyllaceae	*Nama hispidum*	purple mat
	Phacelia arizonica	Arizona scorpionweed
	Phacelia integrifolia	gypsum scorpion-weed
Iridaceae	*Sisyrinchium demissum*	dwarf blue-eyed grass
	Sisyrinchium montanum	mountain blue eyedgrass
Juncaceae	*Juncus arcticus*	arctic rush
	Juncus arcticus var. *balticus*	
	Juncus balticus	Baltic rush
	Juncus ensifolius	swordleaf rush
Lamiaceae	*Hedeoma drummondii*	Drummond's false pennyroyal
	Marrubium vulgare	horehound
	Monarda punctata ssp. *punctata*	spotted beebalm
Linaceae	*Linum aristatum*	bristle flax
	Linum puberulum	desert flax
Loasaceae	*Mentzelia multiflora* var. *multiflora*	Adonis blazingstar
	Mentzelia pumila	dwarf blazingstar
	Mentzelia strictissima	grassland blazingstar
Malvaceae	*Malva neglecta*	cheeseweed
	Sphaeralcea coccinea ssp. *coccinea*	scarlet globe-mallow
	Sphaeralcea fendleri	Fendler's globemallow
	Sphaeralcea incana	gray globemallow
Nyctaginaceae	*Mirabilis linearis*	linearleaf four-o'clock
	Mirabilis multiflora	Colorado four o'clock
Oleaceae	*Forestiera pubescens* var. *pubescens*	New Mexico olive
Onagraceae	*Calylophus hartwegii* ssp. *fendleri*	Hartweg's sundrops
	Gaura coccinea	scarlet gaura
	Oenothera albicaulis	white-stem evening primrose
	Oenothera coronopifolia	crownleaf evening primrose
	Oenothera pallida	pale evening primrose
Orobanchaceae	*Conopholis alpina* var. *mexicana*	alpine squawroot
Pinaceae	*Pinus edulis*	pinyon pine
	Pinus ponderosa	ponderosa pine
Plantaginaceae	*Plantago major*	broadleaf plantain
	Plantago patagonica	woolly plantain
Poaceae	*Achnatherum hymenoides*	Indian ricegrass
	Alopecurus aequalis	short foxtail
	Andropogon gerardii	big bluestem
	Andropogon hallii	sand bluestem
	Aristida purpurea var. *fendleriana*	Fendler's threeawn

Family	Species	Common name
Appendix B, continued.		
	Aristida purpurea var. *purpurea*	purple threeawn
	Bouteloua curtipendula	sideoats grama
	Bouteloua eriopoda	black grama
	Bouteloua gracilis	blue grama
	Bouteloua hirsuta	hairy grama
	Bromus carinatus	California brome
	Bromus catharticus	rescue brome
	Bromus inermis	awnless brome
	Bromus tectorum	cheat grass
	Distichlis spicata	desert saltgrass
	Elymus elymoides	bottlebrush squirreltail
	Elymus repens	quackgrass
	Hesperostipa comata	needleandthread
	Hesperostipa neomexicana	New Mexico needlegrass
	Hordeum jubatum	foxtail barley
	Koeleria macrantha	junegrass
	Lycurus phleoides	wolftail
	Muhlenbergia andina	foxtail muhly
	Muhlenbergia asperifolia	scratchgrass
	Muhlenbergia pauciflora	New Mexico muhly
	Muhlenbergia porteri	bush muhly
	Muhlenbergia pungens	sandhill muhly
	Muhlenbergia repens	creeping muhly
	Muhlenbergia richardsonis	mat muhly
	Muhlenbergia torreyi	ring muhly
	Pascopyrum smithii	western wheatgrass
	Pleuraphis jamesii	galleta
	Poa nemoralis ssp. *interior*	inland bluegrass
	Poa pratensis	Kentucky bluegrass
	Polypogon monspeliensis	annual rabbitsfoot grass
	Schizachyrium scoparium var. *scoparium*	little bluestem
	Setaria vulpiseta	plains bristlegrass
	Sporobolus contractus	spike dropseed
	Sporobolus cryptandrus	sand dropseed
	Sporobolus flexuosus	mesa dropseed
	Sporobolus giganteus	giant dropseed
Polemoniaceae	*Ipomopsis longiflora* ssp. *longiflora*	flaxflowered ipomopsis
	Ipomopsis multiflora	manyflowered ipomopsis
Polygalaceae	*Polygala alba*	white milkwort
	Eriogonum annuum	annual buckwheat
	Eriogonum tenellum	matted wildbuckwheat
	Rumex crispus	curly dock
Ranunculaceae	*Clematis ligusticifolia*	western white clematis
	Ranunculus cymbalaria	alkali buttercup

Appendix B, continued.

Family	Species	Common name
	Ranunculus macounii	Macoun buttercup
Rosaceae	*Cercocarpus montanus*	alderleaf mountain mahogany
	Fallugia paradoxa	Apache plume
	Prunus virginiana var. *melanocarpa*	black chokecherry
	Rosa woodsii	Woods' rose
Rubiaceae	*Houstonia rubra*	red bluet
Salicaceae	*Populus deltoides ssp. wislizeni*	Rio Grande cottonwood
	Populus fremontii	Fremont's cottonwood
	Populus X acuminata	lanceleaf cottonwood
	Salix amygdaloides	peachleaf willow
	Salix gooddingii	Goodding's willow
	Salix lucida ssp. lasiandra	Pacific willow
	Salix lutea	yellow willow
Saururaceae	*Anemopsis californica*	yerba mansa
Scrophulariaceae	*Castilleja integra*	wholeleaf Indian paintbrush
	Cordylanthus wrightii	Wright bird's-beak
	Mimulus glabratus	smooth monkeyflower
	Penstemon crandallii	Crandall's beardtongue
	Penstemon virgatus	upright blue beardtongue
	Veronica anagallis-aquatica	water speedwell
Solanaceae	*Chamaesaracha coronopus*	greenleaf five eyes
	Lycium pallidum	pale desert-thorn
	Physalis hederifolia var. *comata*	ivyleaf groundcherry
	Physalis hederifolia var. *fendleri*	Fendler's groundcherry
	Solanum elaeagnifolium	silverleaf nightshade
	Solanum ptychanthum	West Indian nightshade
Tamaricaceae	*Tamarix chinensis*	Chinese saltcedar
Typhaceae	*Typha domingensis*	southern cattail
Ulmaceae	*Ulmus pumila*	Siberian elm
Verbenaceae	*Glandularia bipinnatifida*	Dakota mock vervain
	Glandularia quandrangulata	beaked mock vervain
	Glandularia racemosa	pale mock vervain
	Glandularia wrightii	DavisbMountain mock vervain
	Verbena bracteata	bigbract verbena
	Verbena macdougalii	MacDougal verbena
Viscaceae	*Phoradendron juniperinum*	juniper mistletoe
Vitaceae	*Parthenocissus quinquefolia*	American ivy
	Parthenocissus vitacea	Virginia creeper

Appendix C. Exotic Plant Species List By Grid Cell

Appendix C is the exotic species list by grid cell in Salinas Pueblo Missions National Monument. The 125 grid cells were approximately two ha each. We identified land use types by dominant species and physical land attributes. There are three park units at Salinas Pueblo Missions National Monument: Abo (36 grid cells), Gran Quivira (77 grid cells), and Quarai (12 grid cells). We identified land cover types by dominant species and physical land attributes. The eight land cover types were: Grassland (12 grid cells), Pinyon-Juniper Woodland (39 grid cells), Pinyon-Juniper Woodland and Savanna (60 grid cells), Riparian (3 grid cells), Riparian Shrubland (1 grid cell), Shrubland (5 grid cells), Sparsely Vegetated (3 grid cells), and Urban (2 grid cells).

Grid cell	Park unit	Land cover type	Species	Common name
3	Abo	PJ Woodland and Savanna	Kochia scoparia	kochia
4	Abo	PJ Woodland	Melilotus officinalis	yellow sweetclover
11	Abo	PJ Woodland and Savanna	Carduus nutans	odding plumeless thistle
11	Abo	PJ Woodland and Savanna	Rumex crispus	curly dock
20	Abo	Grassland	Erodium cicutarium	redstem stork's bill
20	Abo	Grassland	Kochia scoparia	kochia
20	Abo	Grassland	Poa pratensis	Kentucky bluegrass
21	Abo	PJ Woodland and Savanna	Melilotus officinalis	yellow sweetclover
21	Abo	PJ Woodland and Savanna	Tamarix spp.	tamarisk
21	Abo	PJ Woodland and Savanna	Taraxacum officinale	common dandelion
25	Abo	Grassland	Erodium cicutarium	redstem stork's bill
25	Abo	Grassland	Kochia scoparia	kochia
25	Abo	Grassland	Salsola tragus	prickly Russian thistle
26	Abo	Grassland	Convolvulus arvensis	field bindweed
26	Abo	Grassland	Eleusine indica	goose grass
26	Abo	Grassland	Kochia scoparia	kochia
26	Abo	Grassland	Marrubium vulgare	horehound
26	Abo	Grassland	Melilotus officinalis	yellow sweetclover
26	Abo	Grassland	Salsola tragus	prickly Russian thistle
26	Abo	Grassland	Tamarix spp.	tamarisk
26	Abo	Grassland	Ulmus pumila	Siberian elm
27	Abo	PJ Woodland and Savanna	Salsola tragus	prickly Russian thistle
27	Abo	PJ Woodland and Savanna	Tragopogon dubius	western goat's beard
27	Abo	PJ Woodland and Savanna	Ulmus pumila	Siberian elm
31	Abo	Grassland	Poa pratensis	Kentucky bluegrass
33	Abo	PJ Woodland and Savanna	Salsola tragus	prickly Russian thistle
39	Abo	Grassland	Kochia scoparia	kochia
46	Abo	PJ Woodland	Kochia scoparia	kochia
50	Abo	Riparian	Bromus catharticus	rescue brome
50	Abo	Riparian	Convolvulus arvensis	field bindweed
50	Abo	Riparian	Erodium cicutarium	redstem stork's bill
50	Abo	Riparian	Marrubium vulgare	horehound
50	Abo	Riparian	Melilotus officinalis	yellow sweetclover
50	Abo	Riparian	Rumex crispus	curly dock
50	Abo	Riparian	Sisymbrium altissimum	Jim Hill mustard

Appendix C, continued.

Grid cell	Park unit	Land cover type	Species	Common name
50	Abo	Riparian	*Tamarix* spp.	tamarisk
50	Abo	Riparian	*Taraxacum officinale*	common dandelion
50	Abo	Riparian	*Tragopogon dubius*	western goat's beard
53	Abo	Riparian Shrubland	*Bromus catharticus*	rescue brome
53	Abo	Riparian Shrubland	*Marrubium vulgare*	horehound
53	Abo	Riparian Shrubland	*Melilotus officinalis*	yellow sweetclover
53	Abo	Riparian Shrubland	*Rumex crispus*	curly dock
53	Abo	Riparian Shrubland	*Tamarix* spp.	tamarisk
59	Abo	PJ Woodland and Savanna	*Salsola tragus*	prickly Russian thistle
61	Abo	PJ Woodland and Savanna	*Kochia scoparia*	kochia
63	Abo	PJ Woodland and Savanna	*Salsola tragus*	prickly Russian thistle
71	Gran Quivira	PJ Woodland and Savanna	*Marrubium vulgare*	horehound
82	Gran Quivira	PJ Woodland and Savanna	*Marrubium vulgare*	horehound
103	Gran Quivira	PJ Woodland and Savanna	*Marrubium vulgare*	horehound
111	Gran Quivira	Shrubland	*Marrubium vulgare*	horehound
112	Gran Quivira	Shrubland	*Marrubium vulgare*	horehound
122	Gran Quivira	Shrubland	*Marrubium vulgare*	horehound
123	Gran Quivira	Shrubland	*Marrubium vulgare*	horehound
124	Gran Quivira	Shrubland	*Marrubium vulgare*	horehound
138	Gran Quivira	PJ Woodland	*Marrubium vulgare*	horehound
170	Gran Quivira	Urban	*Marrubium vulgare*	horehound
183	Quarai	PJ Woodland	*Bromus japonicus*	Japanese brome
183	Quarai	PJ Woodland	*Rumex crispus*	curly dock
183	Quarai	PJ Woodland	*Salsola tragus*	prickly Russian thistle
187	Quarai	Grassland	*Convolvulus arvensis*	field bindweed
187	Quarai	Grassland	*Kochia scoparia*	kochia
187	Quarai	Grassland	*Malus pumila*	apple tree
187	Quarai	Grassland	*Rumex crispus*	curly dock
187	Quarai	Grassland	*Tragopogon dubius*	western goat's beard
188	Quarai	Grassland	*Kochia scoparia*	kochia
188	Quarai	Grassland	*Salsola tragus*	prickly Russian thistle
191	Quarai	Riparian	*Convolvulus arvensis*	field bindweed
191	Quarai	Riparian	*Erodium cicutarium*	redstem stork's bill
191	Quarai	Riparian	*Kochia scoparia*	kochia
191	Quarai	Riparian	*Melilotus officinalis*	yellow sweetclover
191	Quarai	Riparian	*Poa pratensis*	Kentucky bluegrass
191	Quarai	Riparian	*Tragopogon dubius*	western goat's beard
192	Quarai	Grassland	*Bromus japonicus*	Japanese brome
192	Quarai	Grassland	*Bromus tectorum*	cheat grass
192	Quarai	Grassland	*Convolvulus arvensis*	field bindweed
192	Quarai	Grassland	*Erodium cicutarium*	redstem stork's bill
192	Quarai	Grassland	*Kochia scoparia*	kochia
192	Quarai	Grassland	*Lactuca serriola*	wild lettuce
192	Quarai	*Grassland*	*Poa pratensis*	Kentucky bluegrass

	Appendix C, continued.			
Grid cell	**Park unit**	**Land cover type**	**Species**	**Common name**
192	Quarai	Grassland	*Taraxacum officinale*	common dandelion
192	Quarai	Grassland	*Tragopogon dubius*	Western goat's beard
192	Quarai	Grassland	*Ulmus pumila*	Siberian elm
193	Quarai	PJ Woodland	*Bromus tectorum*	cheat grass
193	Quarai	PJ Woodland	*Erodium cicutarium*	redstem stork's bill
193	Quarai	PJ Woodland	*Malva neglecta*	cheeseweed
193	Quarai	PJ Woodland	*Medicago lupulina*	black medic
193	Quarai	PJ Woodland	*Taraxacum officinale*	common dandelion
197	Quarai	Riparian	*Bromus catharticus*	rescue brome
197	Quarai	Riparian	*Bromus tectorum*	cheat grass
197	Quarai	Riparian	*Convolvulus arvensis*	field bindweed
197	Quarai	Riparian	*Melilotus officinalis*	yellow sweetclover
197	Quarai	Riparian	*Poa pratensis*	Kentucky bluegrass
201	Quarai	PJ Woodland and Savanna	*Convolvulus arvensis*	field bindweed
201	Quarai	PJ Woodland and Savanna	*Salsola tragus*	prickly Russian thistle

Appendix D. Exotic Plant Species Maps

Appendix D contains the maps of species occurrence for each exotic species in Salinas Pueblo Missions National Monument. The maps also show land cover type by grid cells. The data used to make these maps came from the 50-m belt transect data and the grid cell data. We identified land cover types by dominant species and physical land attributes. These six land cover types were: Grassland (12 grid cells), Pinyon-Juniper Woodland (39 grid cells), Pinyon-Juniper Woodland and Savanna (60 grid cells), Riparian (3 grid cells), Riparian Shrubland (1 grid cells), Shrubland (5 grid cells), Sparsely Vegetated (3 grid cells), and Urban (2 grid cells). Each grid cell is approximately two ha (N=125). Belt transects width varied in size depending on land cover type. Grassland belt transects were three meters in width (150 m²), the Pinyon-Juniper Woodland and Savanna belt transects were in four meters in width (200 m²), and all other land cover type belt transects were seven meters in width (350 m²). We calculated the percent exotic cover by first calculating a midpoint for each cover class and then calculating the mean from the midpoint data (N=125).

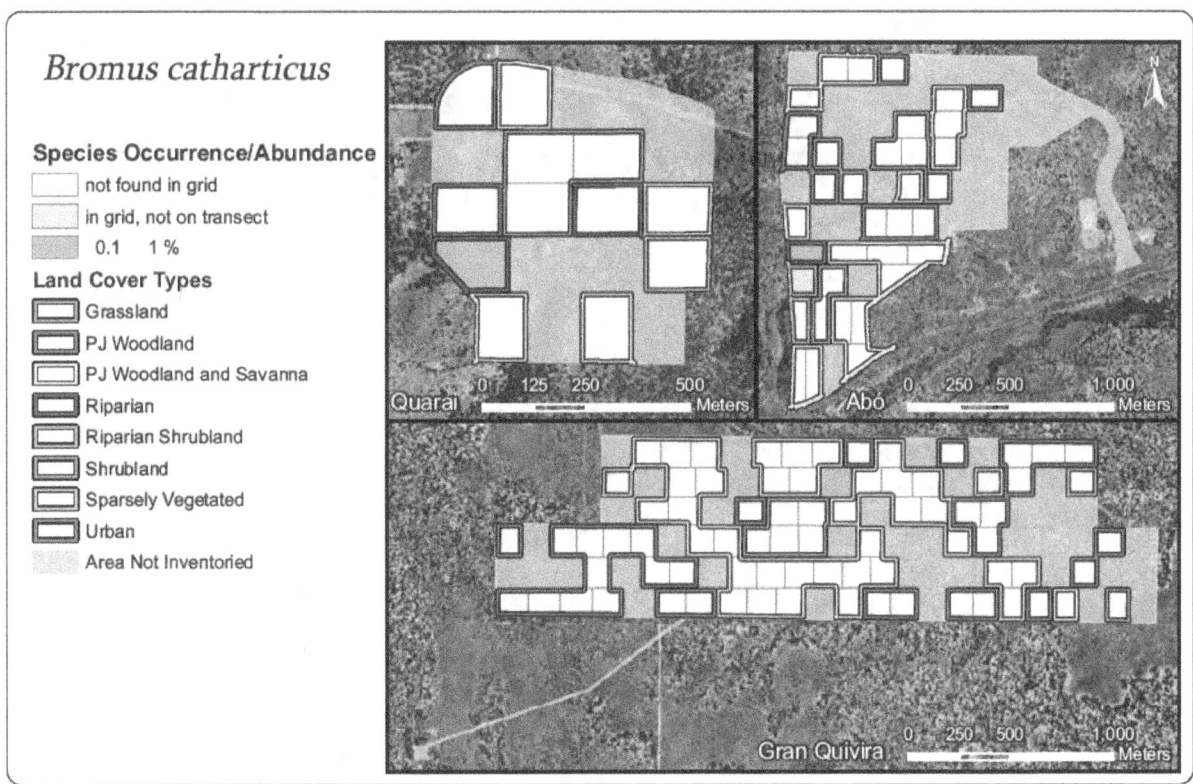

Figure D1. Species occurrence of *Bromus catharticus* by grid cell.

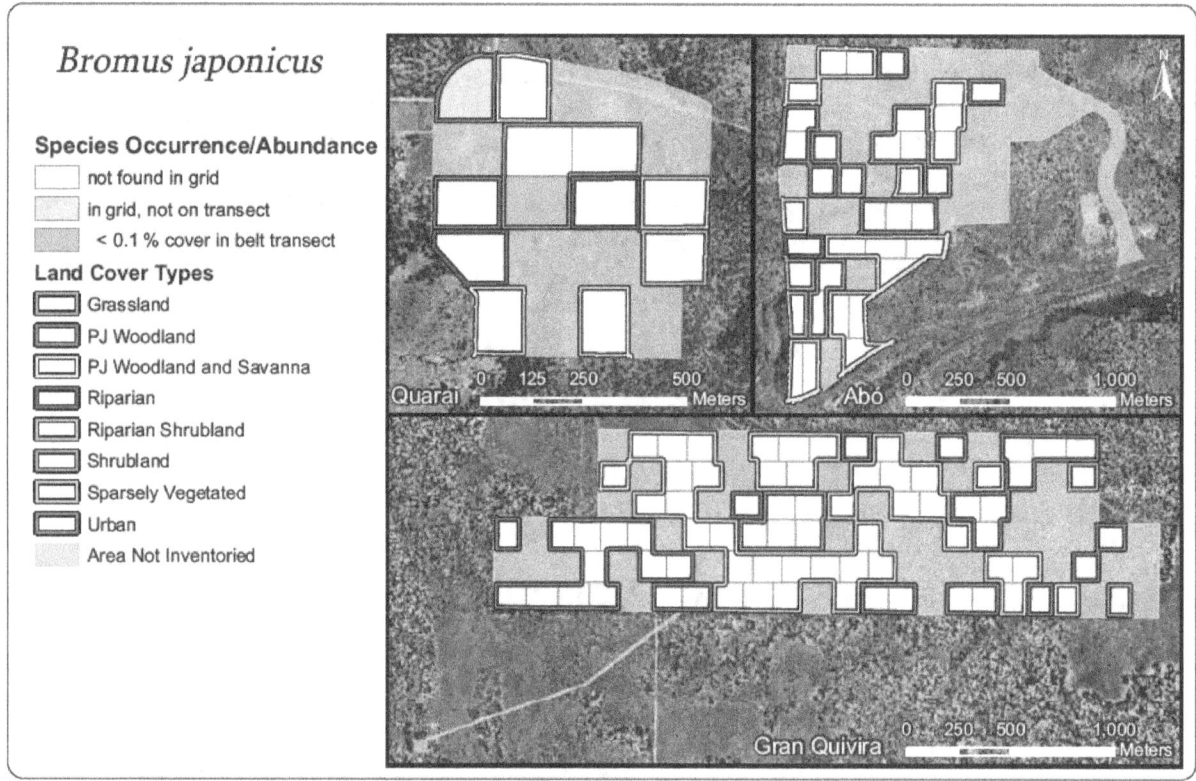

Figure D2. Species occurrence of *Bromus japonicus* by grid cell.

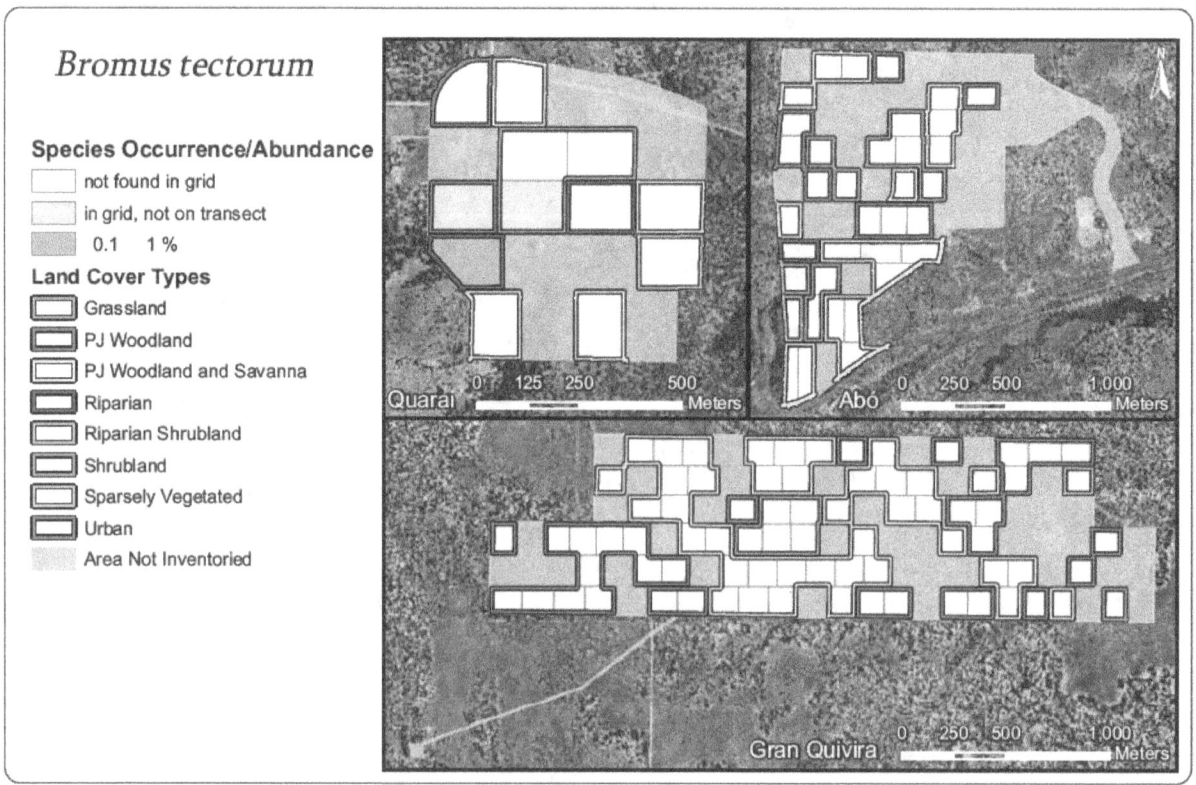

Figure D3. Species occurrence of *Bromus tectorum* by grid cell.

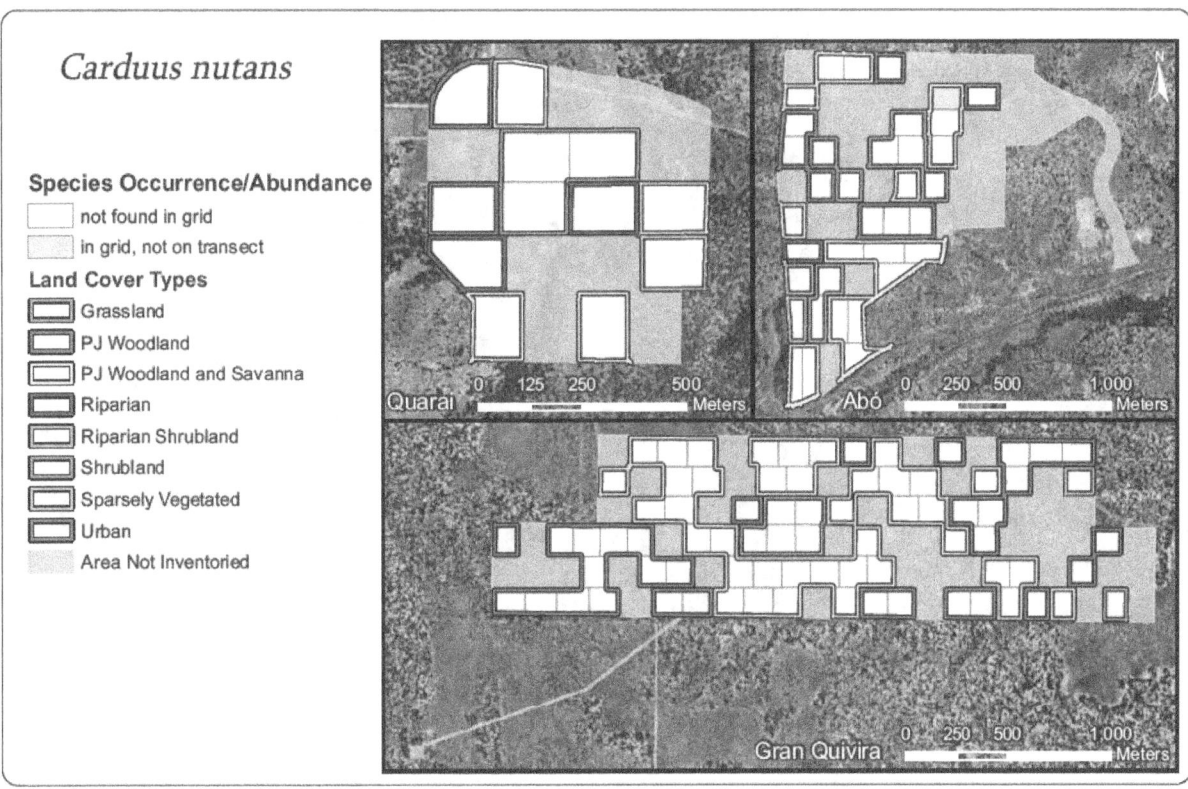

Figure D4. Species occurrence of *Carduus nutans* by grid cell.

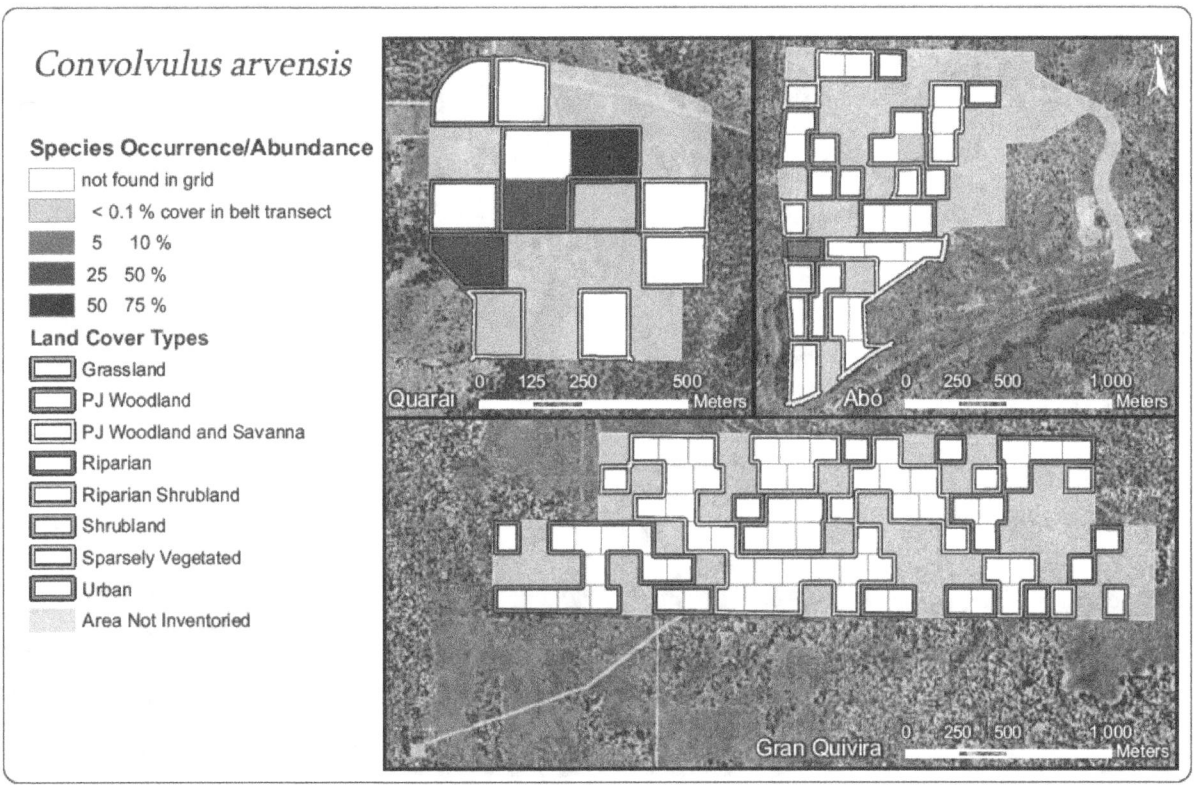

Figure D5. Species occurrence of *Convolvulus arvensis* by grid cell.

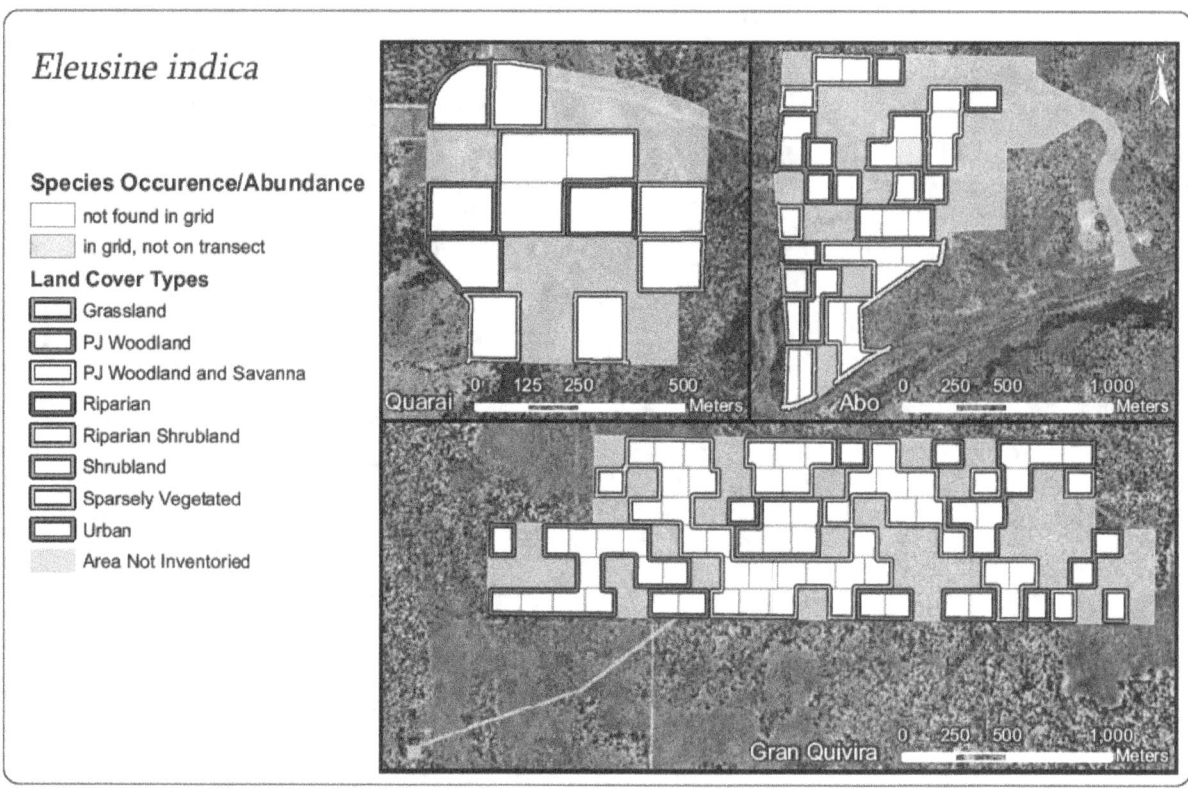

Figure D6. Species occurrence of *Eleusine indica* by grid cell.

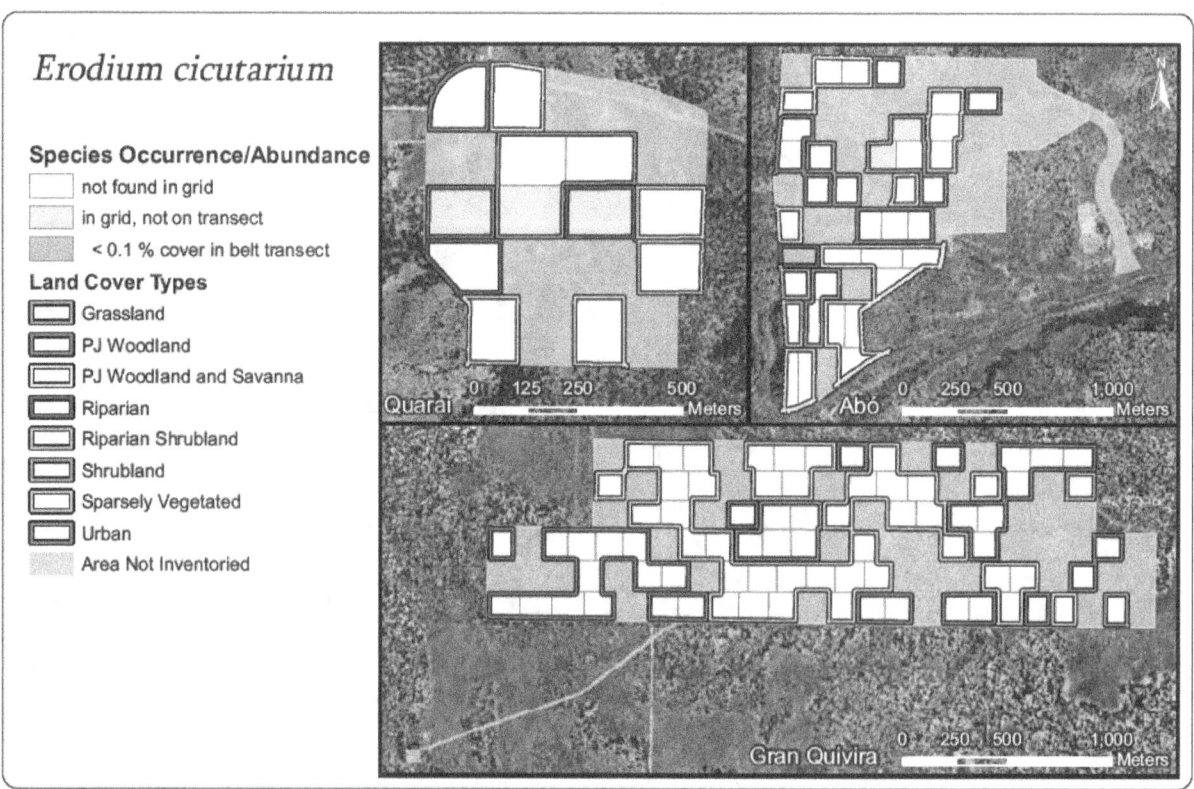

Figure D7. Species occurrence of *Erodium cicutarium* by grid cell.

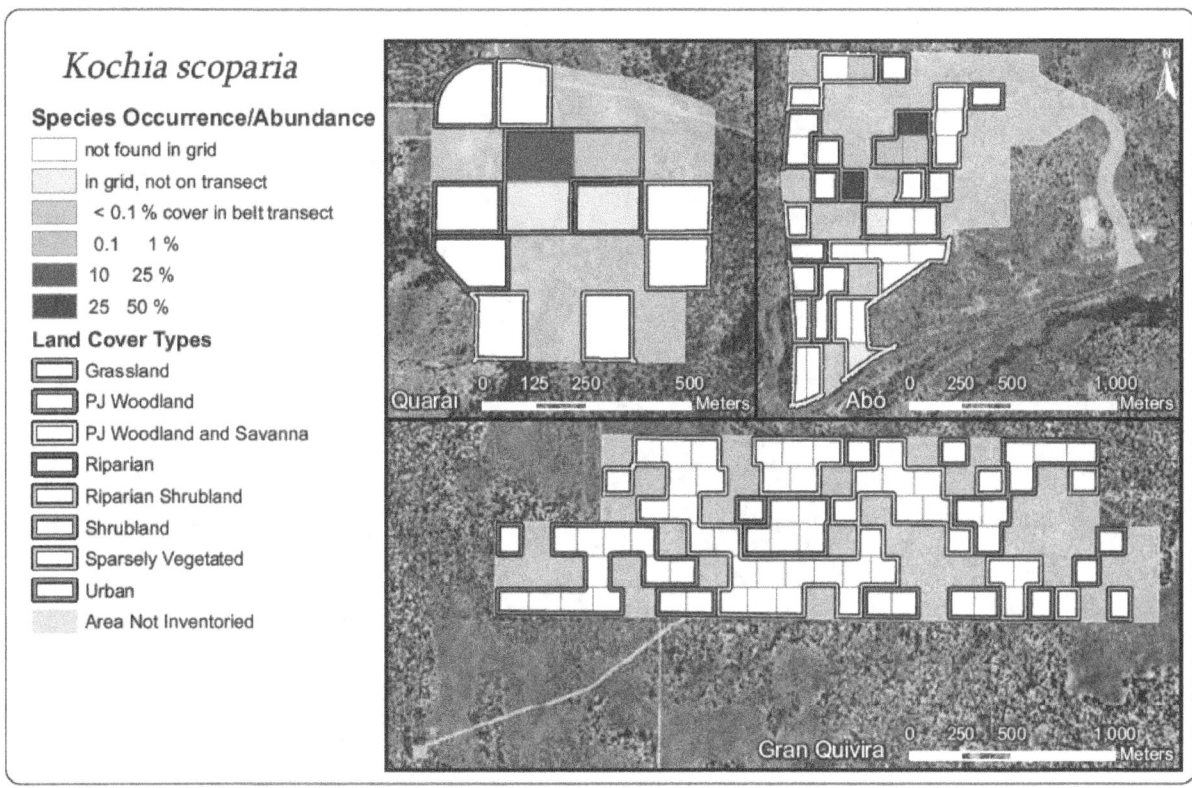

Figure D8. Species occurrence of *Kochia scoparia* by grid cell.

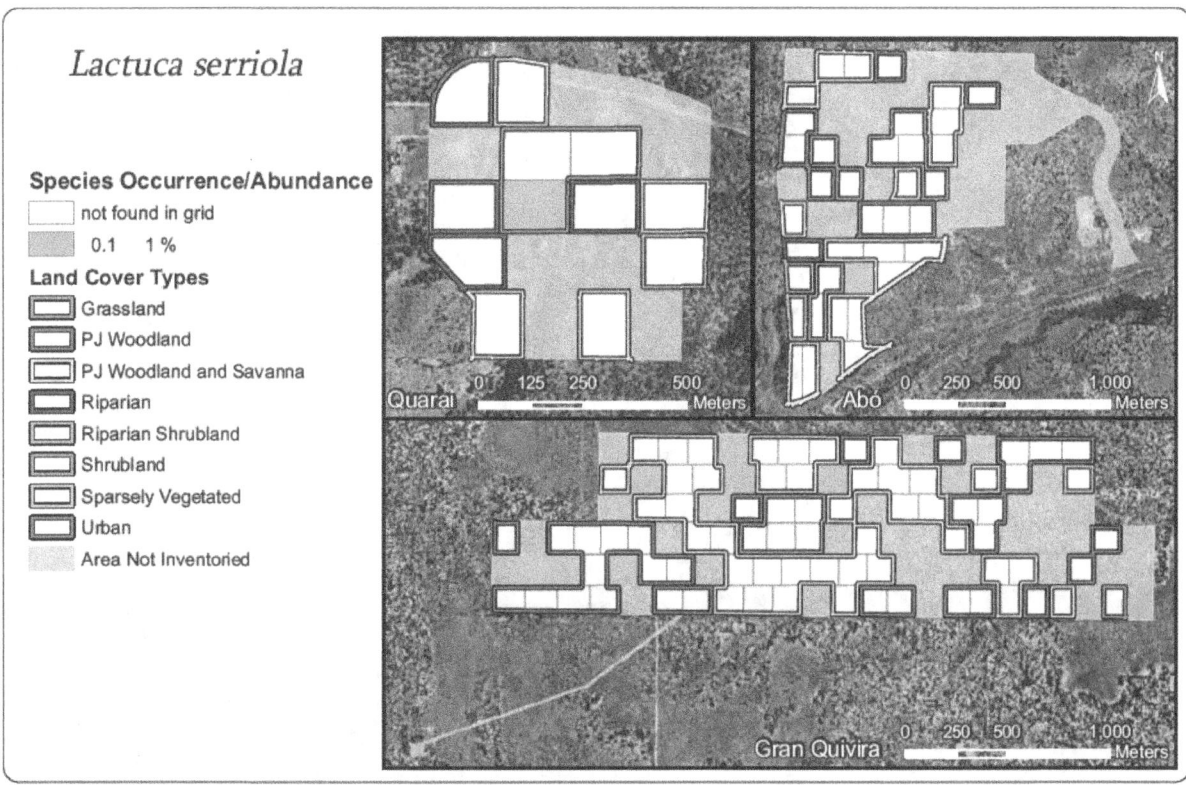

Figure D9. Species occurrence of *Lactuca serriola* by grid cell.

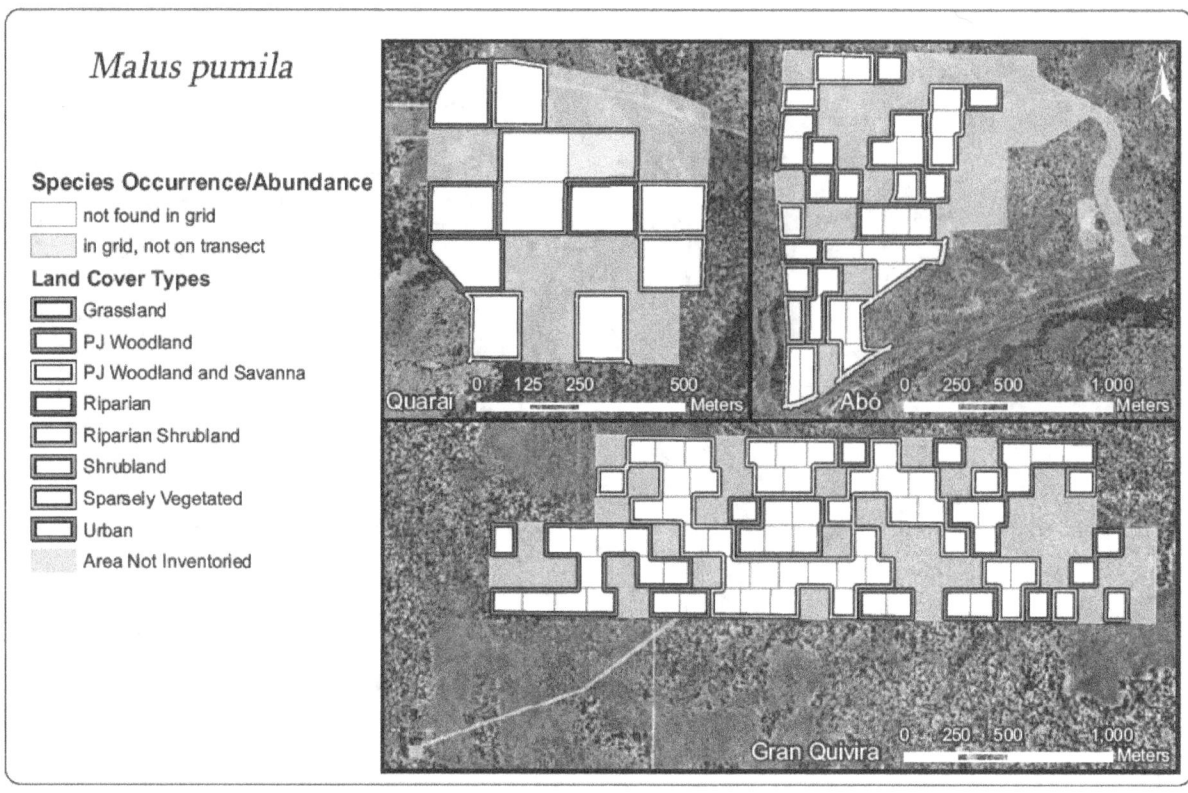

Figure D10. Species occurrence of *Malus pumila* by grid cell.

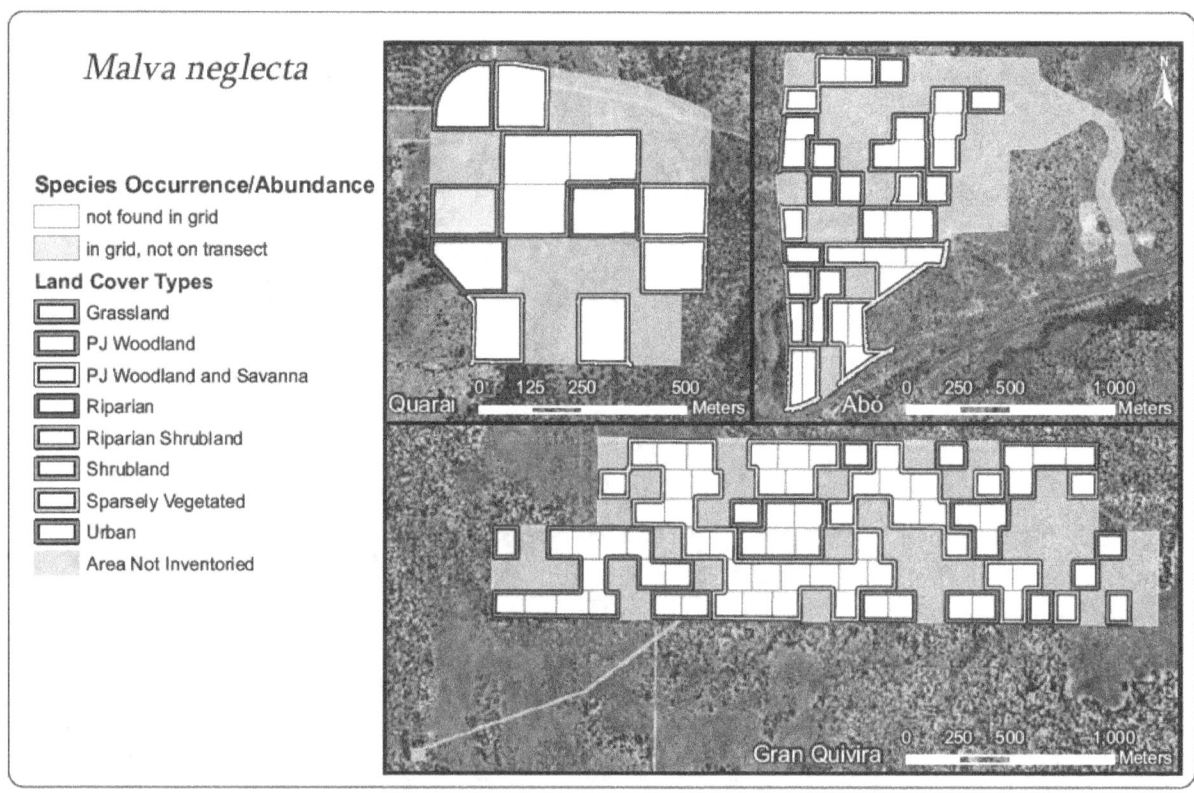

Figure D11. Species occurrence of *Malva neglecta* by grid cell.

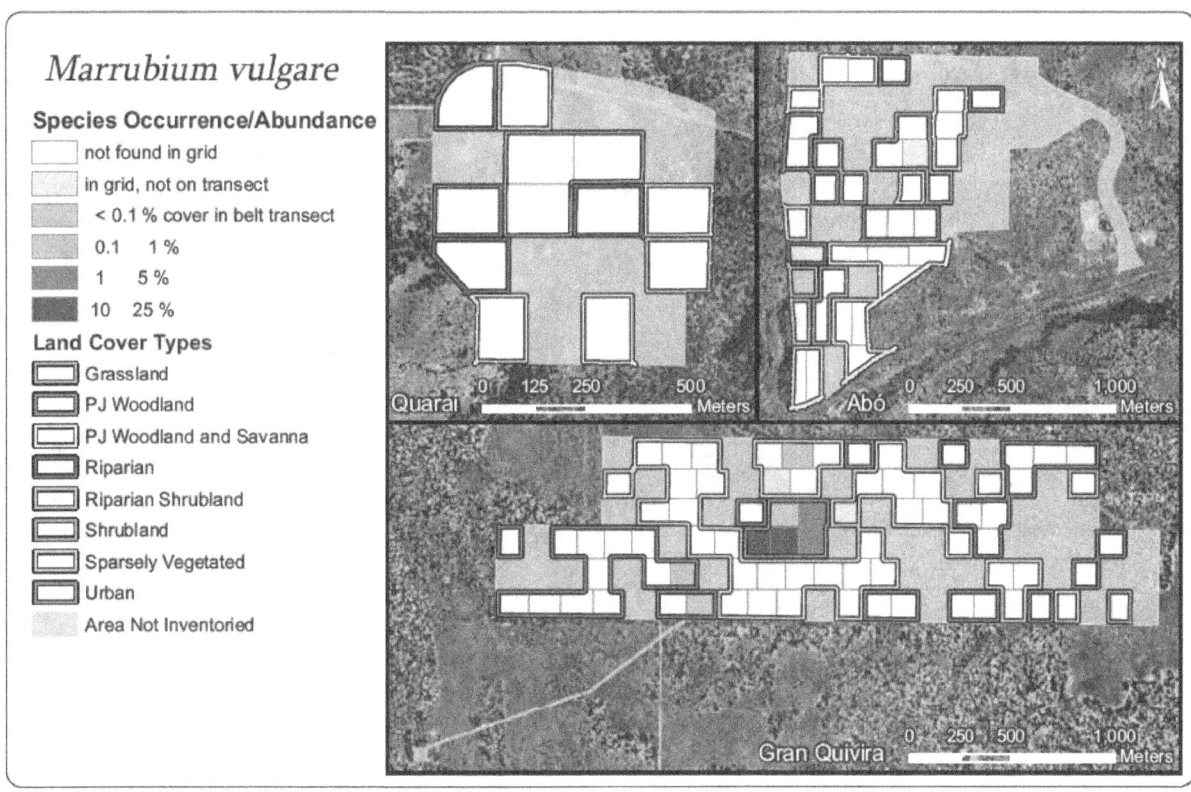

Figure D12. Species occurrence of *Marrubium vulgare* by grid cell.

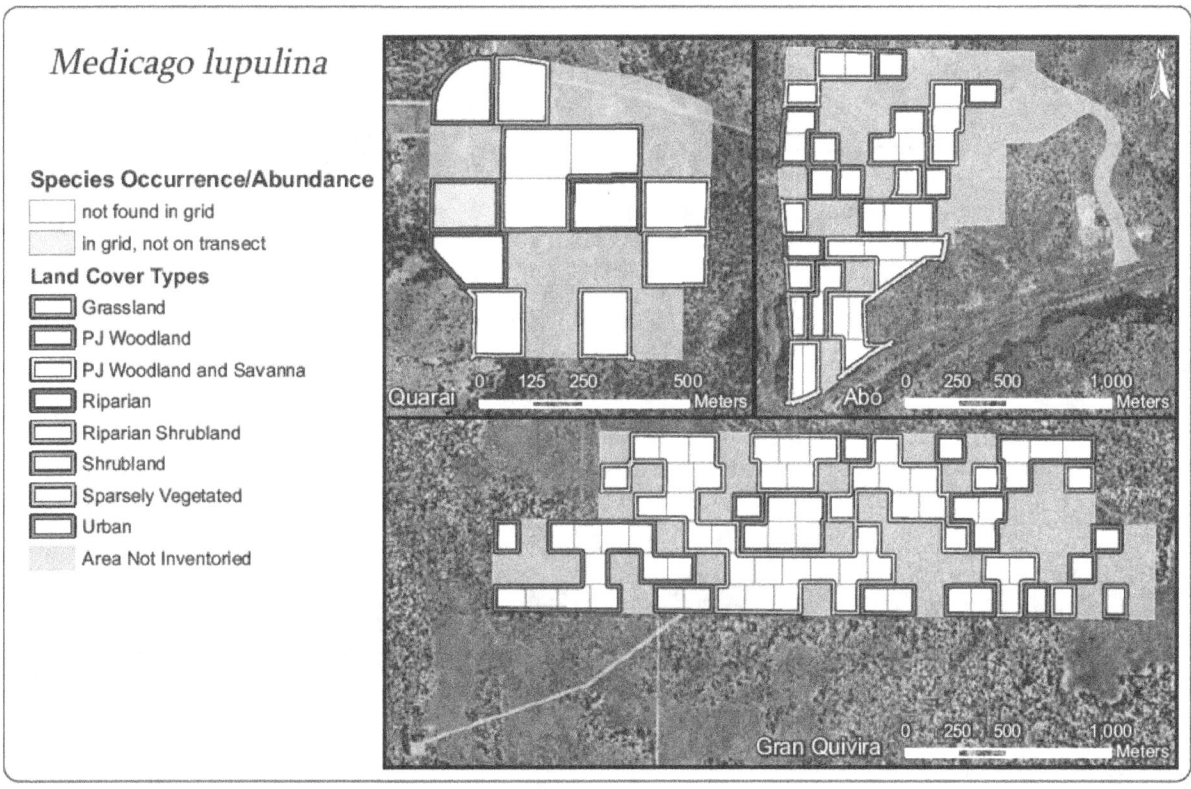

Figure D13. Species occurrence of *Medicago lupulina* by grid cell.

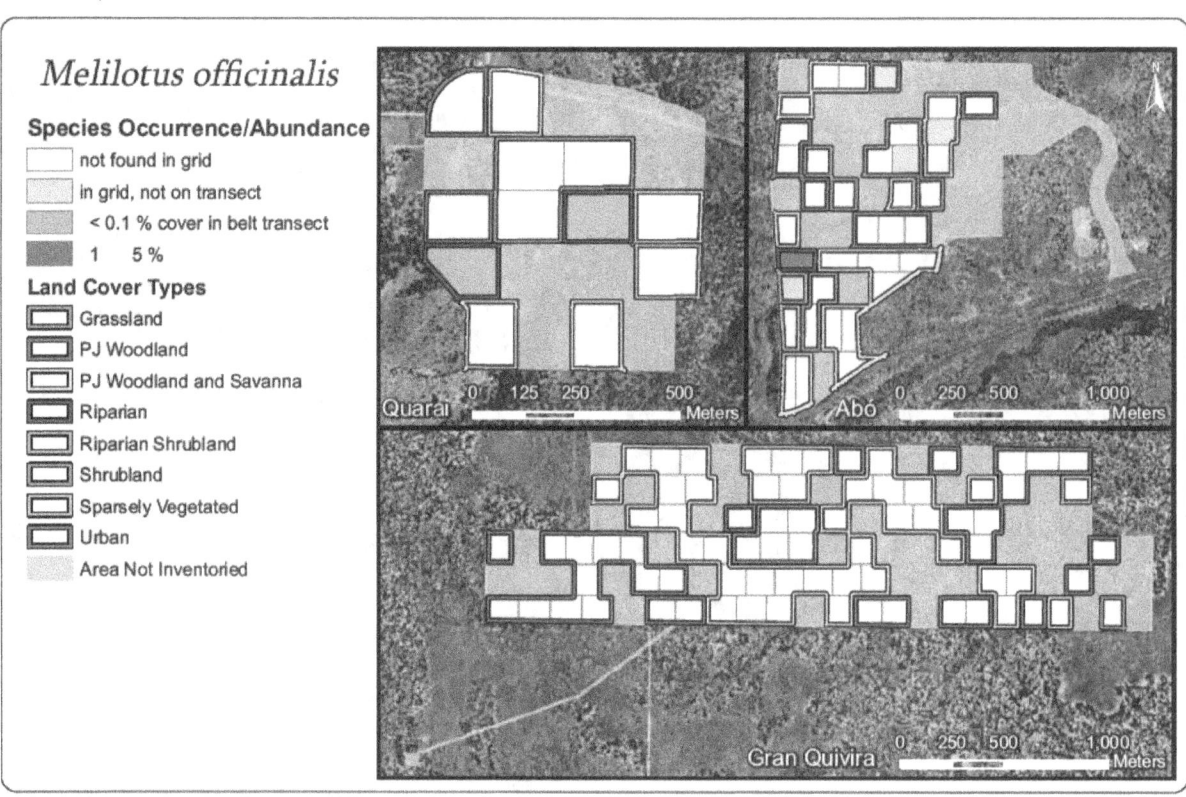

Figure D14. Species occurrence of *Melilotus officinalis* by grid cell.

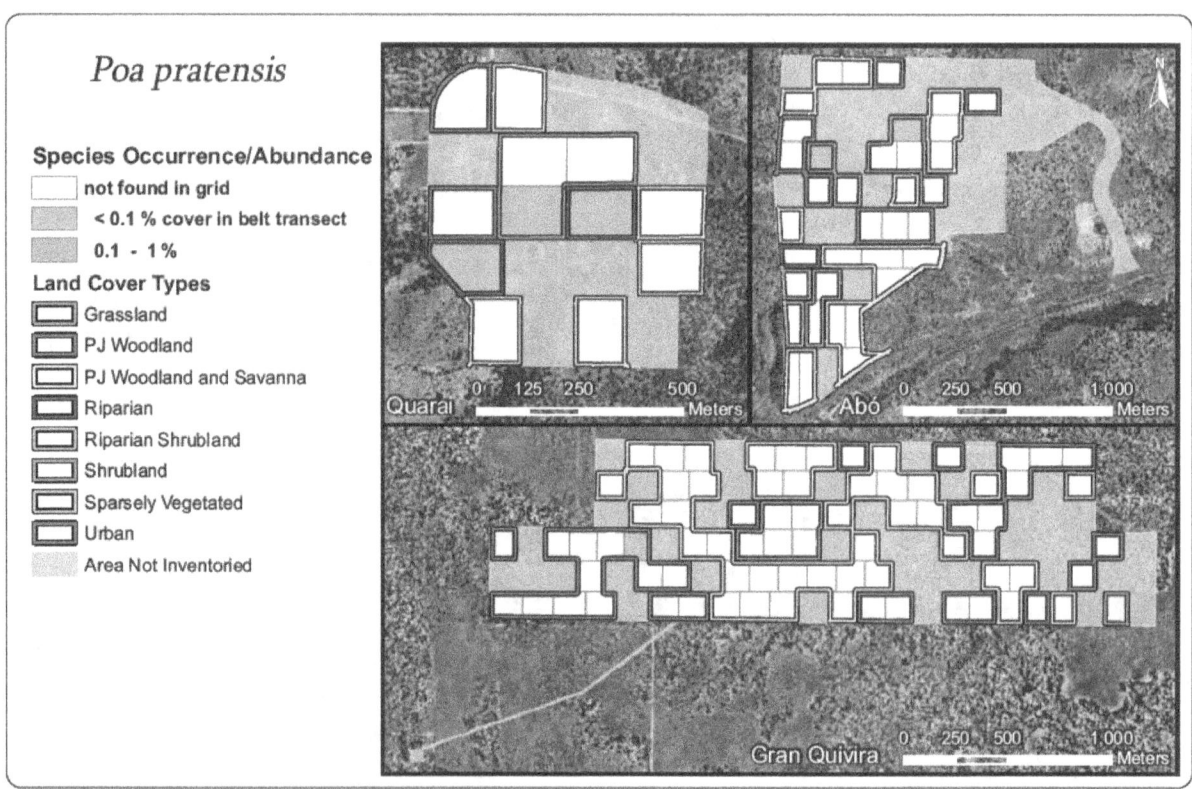

Figure D15. Species occurrence of *Poa pratensis* by grid cell.

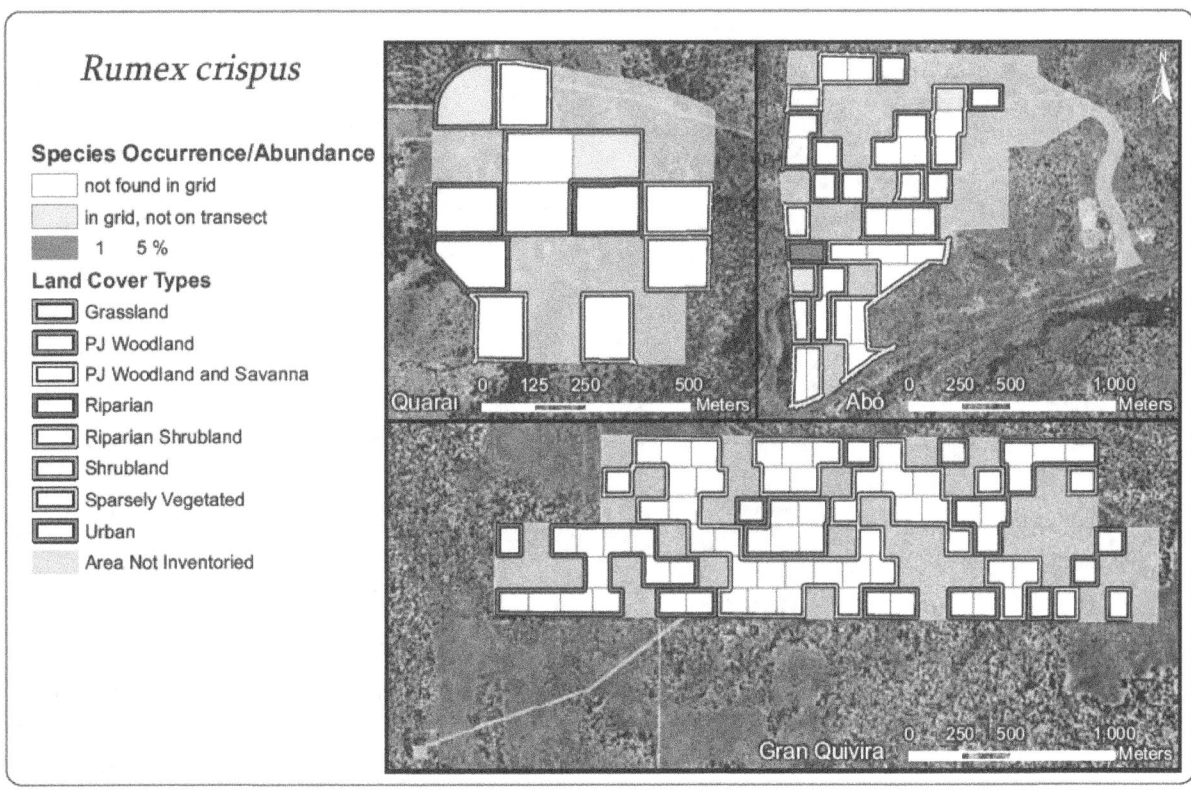

Figure D16. Species occurrence of *Rumex crispus* by grid cell.

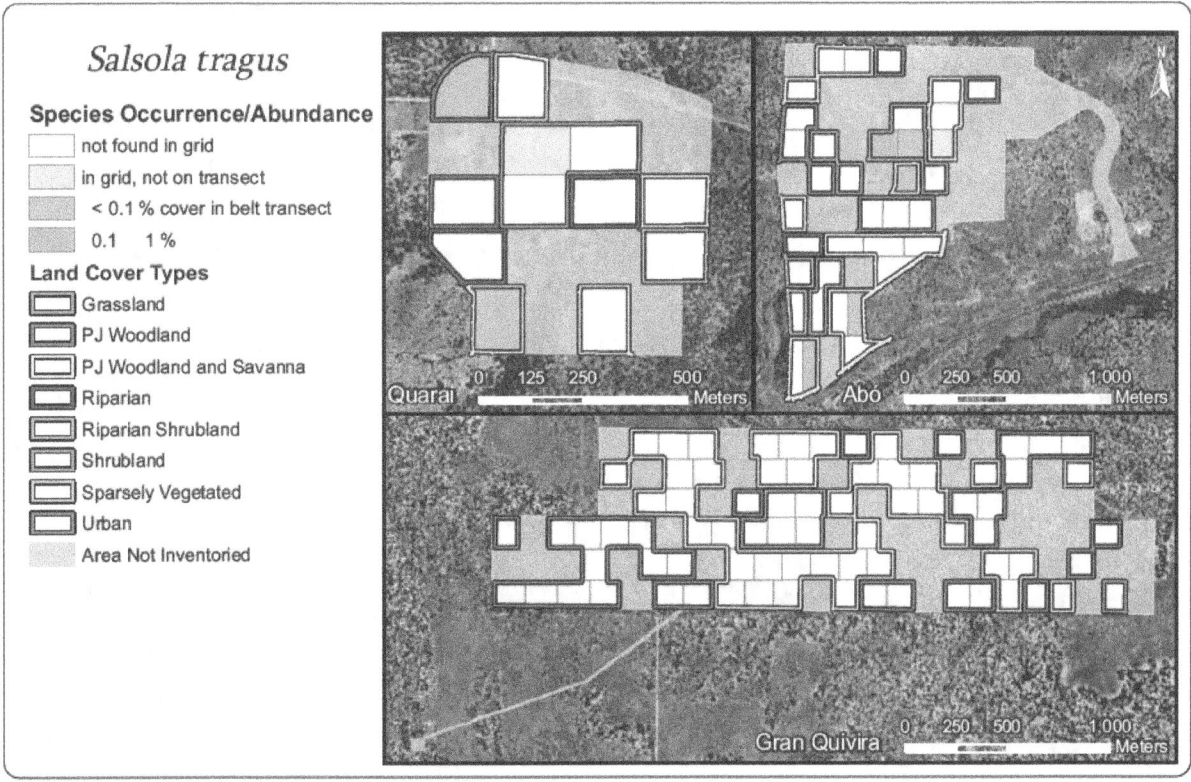

Figure D17. Species occurrence of *Salsola tragus* by grid cell.

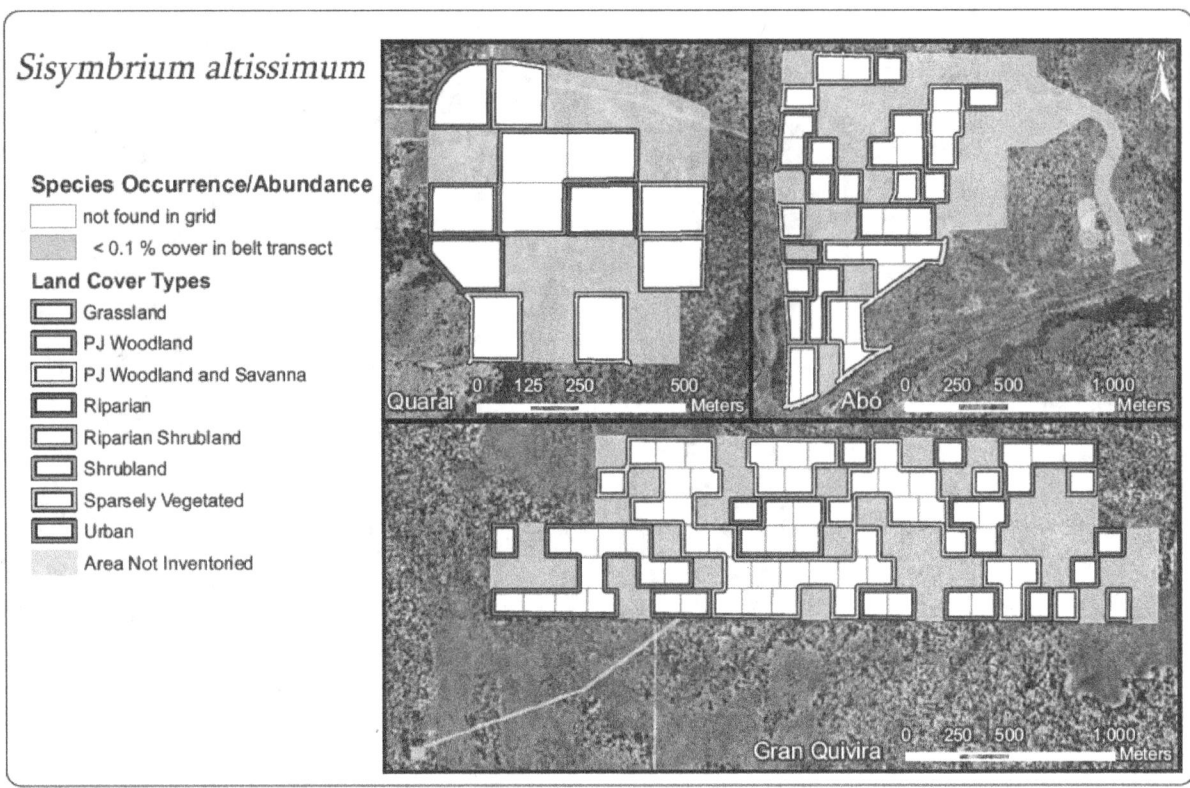

Figure D18. Species occurrence of *Sisymbrium altissimum* by grid cell.

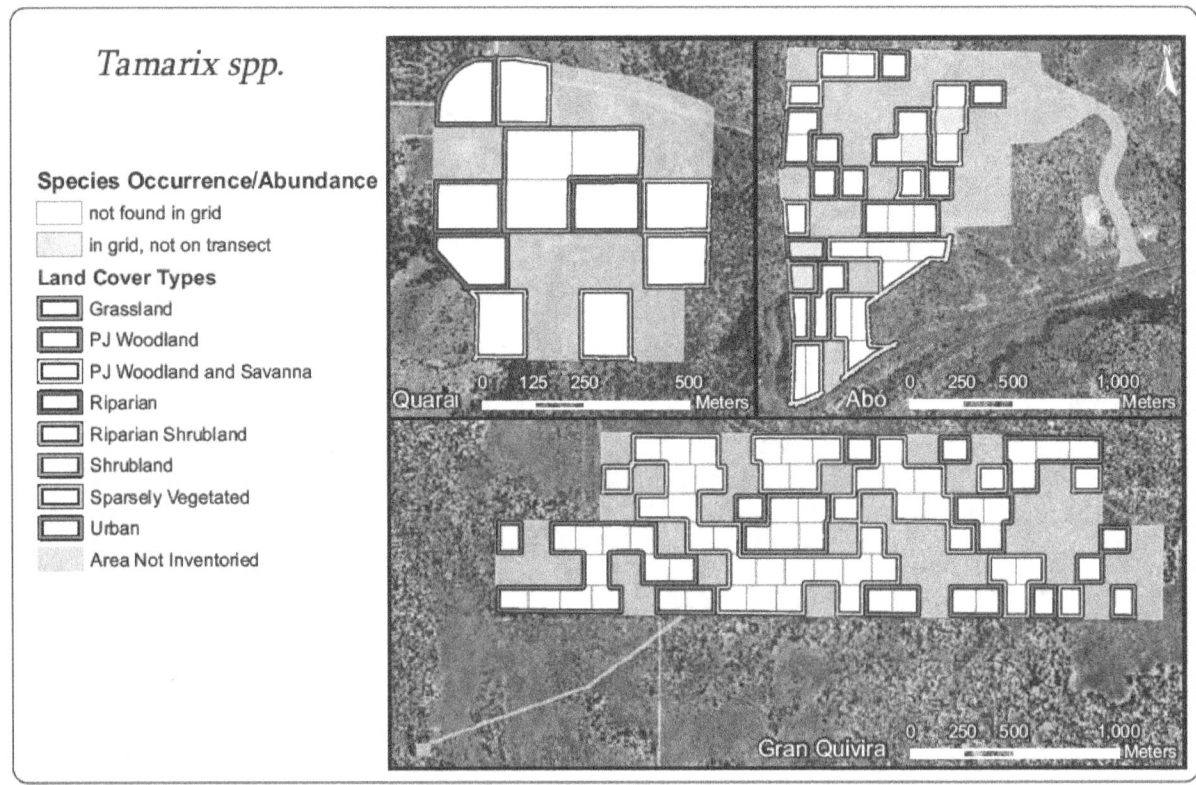

Figure D19. Species occurrence of *Tamarix* spp. by grid cell.

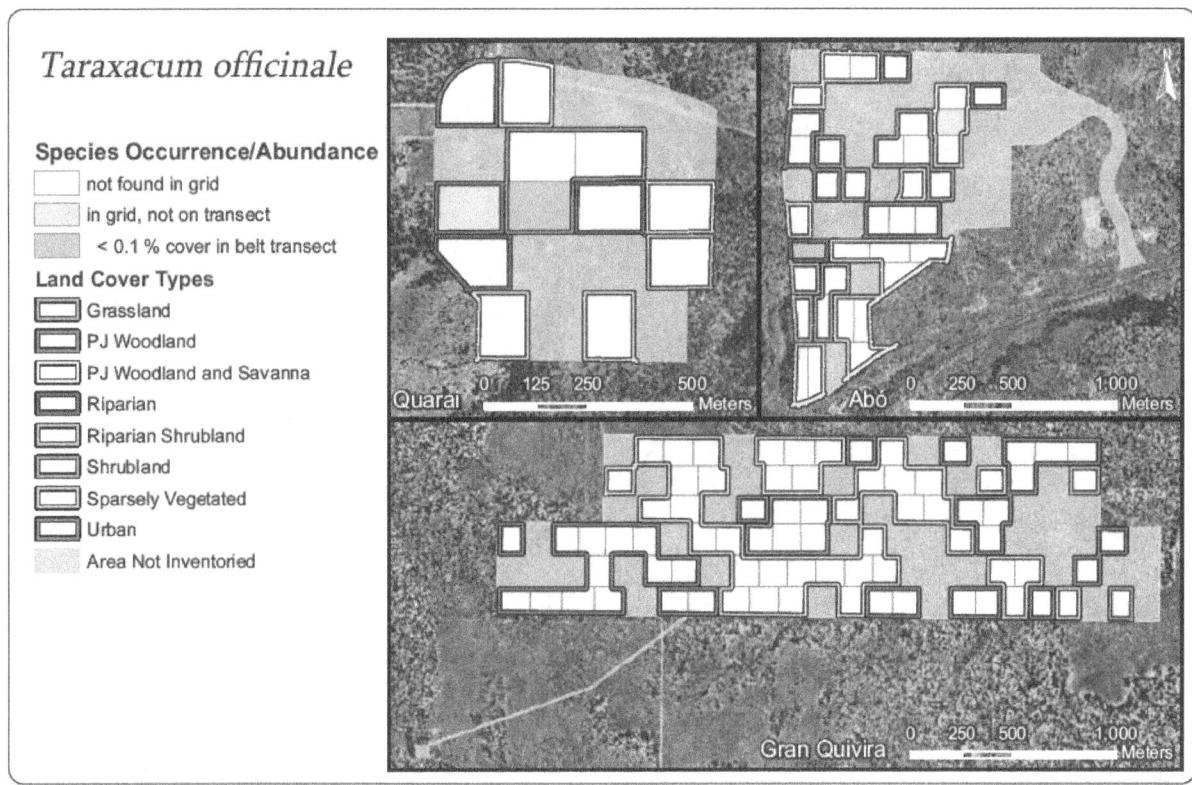

Figure D20. Species occurrence of *Taraxacum officinale* by grid cell.

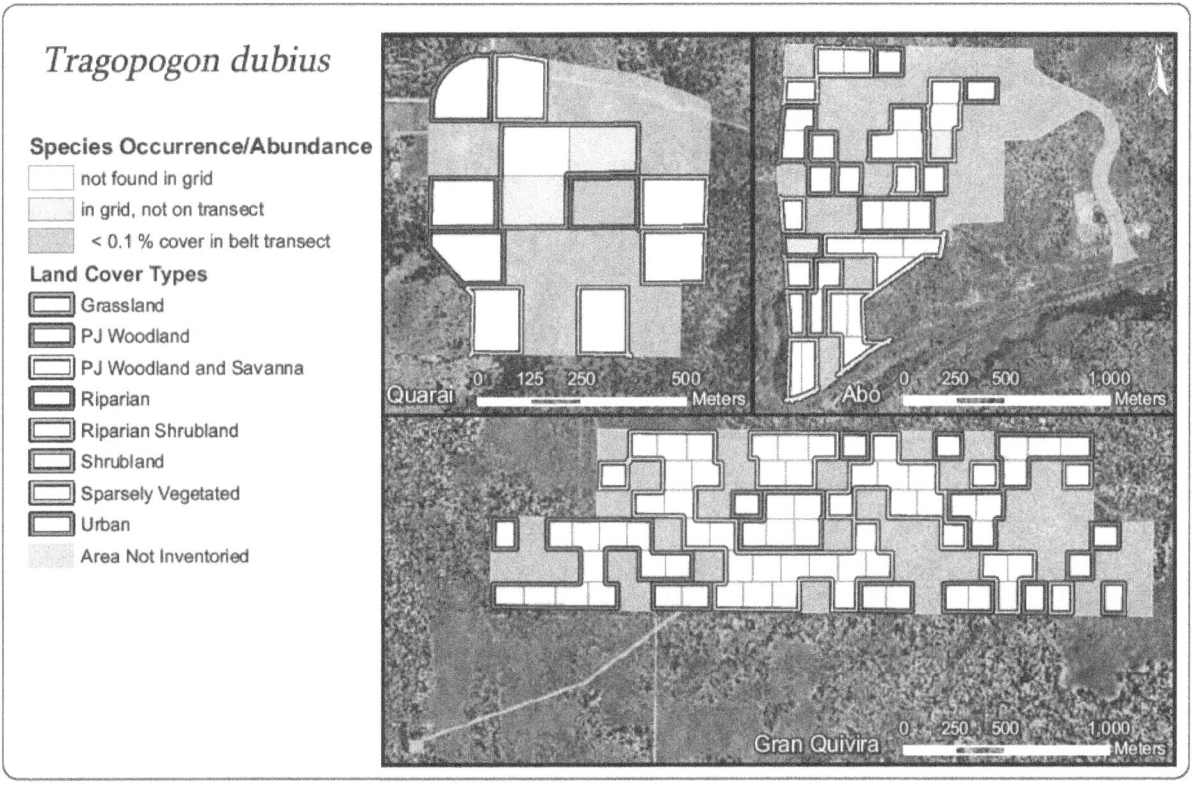

Figure D21. Species occurrence of *Tragopogon dubius* by grid cell.

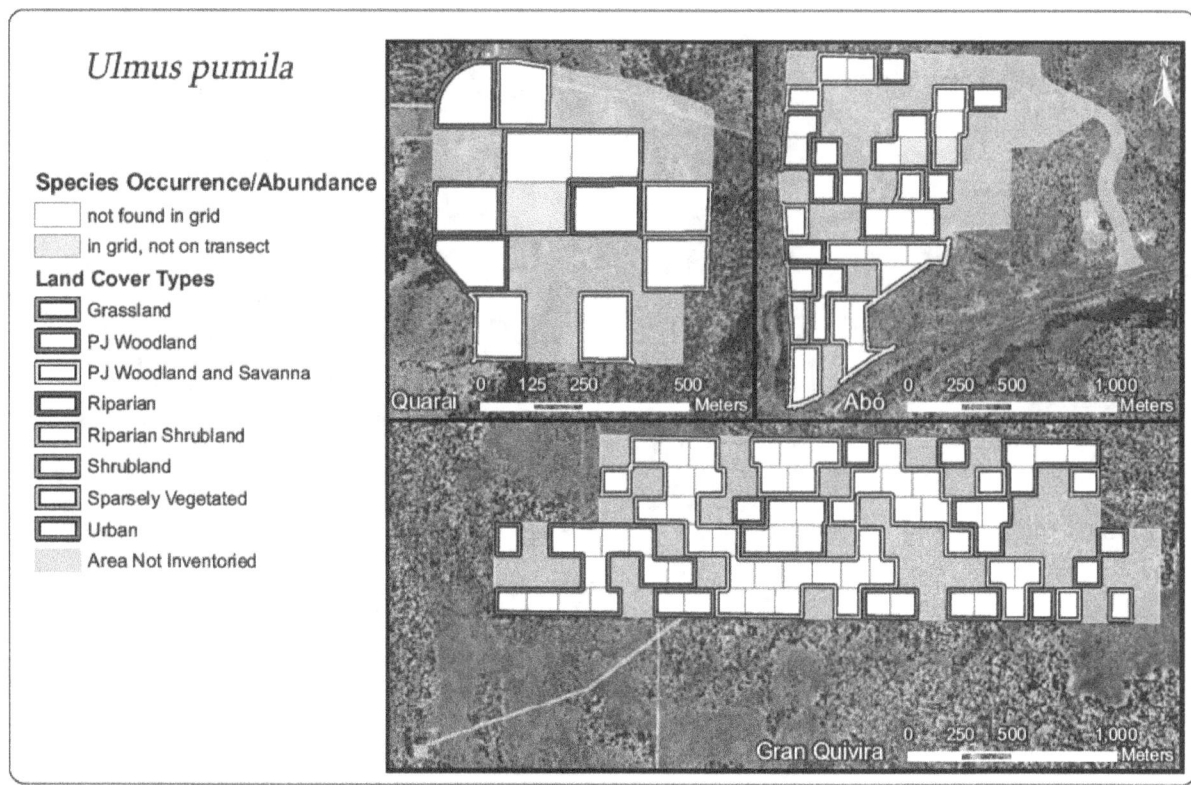

Figure D22. Species occurrence of *Ulmus pumila* by grid cell.

Appendix E. Notes About Transects.

Appendix E contains a list of notes for some grid cell belt transects at Salinas Pueblo Missions National Monument.

Grid cell	Additional comments
17	Transect crosses a shallow wash - no slope collected.
20	Transect crosses a paved trail around the ruins.
21	Edge of arroyo crossed the transect at 49m - successional transects may become shorter due to active erosion. Tamarisk was not flowering so we couldn't determine the species. The invasive spp. was concentrated in the arroyo.
25	Lots of invasive species along the paved pathways.
30	Transect crosses a wash so no slope was recorded.
34	We ran into the park boundary fence. The 0m mark should have been 5m on the otherside of the fence, so the transect was moved in 5m.
39	There is a LOT of *Kochia scoparia* in thie grid cell. All along the ridge and wash in the area. The grid cell is probably around 85% *Kochia scoparia*.
43	This plot was very rocky, there was not much vegetation.
46	The transect crosses the main, paved park entrance road. No data were collected at transect points 25m, 30m, and 35, due to pavement.
48	Steep rocky slope.
49	The transect is along an elevational contour, so no slope was recorded.
50	The transect crosses a drainage so slope really isn't accurate.
53	Lots of rabbitbrush in this transect.
60	Very rocky site, sparse veg.
72	Transect crosses 2-3 small washes/arroyos.
78	Transect runs into boundary fence; the transect is only from 26 to 50m because of this. The 25m point is actually at 26m.
83	The transect has a big dip in the middle (an arroyo) so the slope is a little inaccurate.
92	Transect crosses an access road @ 5.5 to 10.5m.
103	Park access road crosses the transect from 20-44m.
105	Near the equipment storage yard. The access road crosses the transect @ 47-50m.
106	Access road crosses the transect at 16.5m to 20.5m.
107	Access road crosses transect from 20m to 26m.
111	Park paved path intersects transect from 0-3m.
117	The 50m mark was right next to the main park entrance road.
121	Transect crosses a ravine - big dip in the middle.
122	The paved parking lot was in the transect from 45-50m.
123	Lots of *Cholla* spp. in this plot, but it was NOT counted as canopy cover.
124	There is a dip in the middle of the transect due to a small ravine.
137	Near the park entrance road.
138	Transect intersects paved park entrance road at 47m, so there is no point done for 50m (pavement).
144	The transect goes over a hill; the slope is +13 for one half and -13 for the other half. See data sheet for drawing. Also, the whiteboard in these pictures is labelled 126 wrongly.
152	This transect ends in a wash.
160	50m end of the transect is in the bottom of a wash.
169	Some clearing has been done in this grid cell - there are dead branches all over the plot.
170	50m end of the plot is in a wash - sparse vegetation.
182	Lots of cryptobiotic soil crusts.

Appendix E, continued.

Family	Species
183	Large hill in the middle of the transect - that's why no slope or aspect were taken. The transect crossed a well used 4-wheeler track and was very disturbed.
190	Transect crosses a deep, rocky arroyo from 0-34m. Slope from 0-34m = -38%, slope from 34m-50m = -1%
191	191 is just on the edge of a very steep cutbank, the arroyo appears to be actively eroding - note for future sampling.
192	No slope or aspect recorded on datasheet.
193	Lots of brush down along the transect - a tree thinning project is in process.
194	Very rocky slope, sparse vegetation.

The Department of the Interior protects and manages the nation's natural resources and cultural heritage; provides scientific and other information about those resources; and honors its special responsibilities to American Indians, Alaska Natives, and affiliated Island Communities.

NPS 313/106530, January 2011

www.ingramcontent.com/pod-product-compliance
Lightning Source LLC
Chambersburg PA
CBHW080447290526
45791CB00008BA/2638